FOOD
for the
JOURNEY

BOB WALDRON

FOOD
for the
JOURNEY

52 Meditations on the Lord's Supper
to Enrich Your Soul

ELM HILL

A Division of
HarperCollins Christian Publishing

www.elmhillbooks.com

© 2020 Bob Waldron

FOOD for the JOURNEY

All rights reserved. No portion of this book may be reproduced, stored in a retrieval system, or transmitted in any form or by any means—electronic, mechanical, photocopy, recording, scanning, or other—except for brief quotations in critical reviews or articles, without the prior written permission of the publisher.

Published in Nashville, Tennessee, by Elm Hill, an imprint of Thomas Nelson. Elm Hill and Thomas Nelson are registered trademarks of HarperCollins Christian Publishing, Inc.

Cover design by Kristen Ingebretson
Cover photo by Artur Aldyrkhanov on Unsplash

Elm Hill titles may be purchased in bulk for educational, business, fund-raising, or sales promotional use. For information, please e-mail SpecialMarkets@ThomasNelson.com.

All Scripture quotations, unless otherwise indicated, are taken from the Holy Bible, New International Version®, NIV®. © 1973, 1978, 1984, 2011 by Biblica Inc.® Used by permission. All rights reserved worldwide. Other Scripture references are from the following sources: New American Standard Bible® (NASB), © 1960, 1962, 1963, 1968, 1971, 1972, 1973, 1975, 1977, 1995 by The Lockman Foundation. Used by permission. Holy Bible, New Living Translation (NLT), © 1996, 2004, 2015. Used by permission of Tyndale House Publishers Inc., Carol Stream, Illinois 60188. All rights reserved. New Revised Standard Version Bible (NRSV), © 1989, the Division of Christian Education of the National Council of the Churches of Christ in the U.S.A. Used by permission. All rights reserved. Revised Standard Version of the Bible (RSV), © 1946, 1952, 1971 by the Division of Christian Education of the National Council of the Churches of Christ in the U.S.A. Used by permission. All rights reserved.

Library of Congress Cataloging-in-Publication Data

Library of Congress Control Number: 2019919445

ISBN 978-1-400330249 (Paperback)
ISBN 978-1-400331291 (Hardbound)
ISBN 978-1-400330256 (eBook)

TO GINA

*My soul mate, companion,
and the love of my life, with whom
I have been privileged to participate in
the Lord's Supper for many beautiful years.*

Contents

Prologue — ix

1: Food for the Journey — 1
2: More Than a Museum of Memories — 4
3: A Rose by Any Other Name — 7
4: The Lord's Supper As Sacrament — 10
5: The New Passover Lamb — 13
6: Around the World — 16
7: Just a Symbol? — 19
8: The New Exodus — 22
9: All Loves Excelling — 25
10: The Meal of Self-Evaluation — 28
11: His Alone — 31
12: The Table of Mercy — 34
13: The Meal for Honored Guests — 37
14: The New Moses — 40
15: Bride Prices and Ransoms — 43
16: The Together Meal — 46
17: When Wild Winds Blow — 49
18: The Covenant Meal — 52
19: The Day of Atonement — 55
20: The Meal of Reconciliation — 58
21: The High Cost of a Free Gift — 61
22: The New Manna — 64
23: Outside the Camp — 67

Contents

24: Settling for Less	70
25: Knowing Christ	73
26: The Table of Tears	76
27: The Meal That Nourishes	79
28: The Meal of Haste	82
29: The Meal of Purity	85
30: The One-Loaf Meal	88
31: Thanksgiving and Celebration	91
32: The Mountains of Fear and Joy	94
33: The New Creation	97
34: Healing the Shame	100
35: Grace Reigns!	103
36: The Messianic Banquet	106
37: The Lord's Fervent Desire	109
38: Waiting: The Time Between	112
39: The Cosmic Battle	115
40: This Is Holy Ground	118
41: Betrayal at the Table	121
42: Great Expectations	124
43: For the Joy Set before Him	127
44: Scorning the Shame	130
45: The Kiss of Death	133
46: The Lord's Supper As Sacrifice	136
47: Under His Wings	139
48: Crossing on Dry Land	142
49: Water for the Thirsty	145
50: Seeing Jesus More Clearly	148
51: Reservation Guaranteed	151
52: It Is Finished!	154
Acknowledgments	157
Notes	159
Select Bibliography	173
About the Author	177

Prologue

You are invited to go on what I hope will be a fulfilling journey to encounter Christ anew. Our path takes us to the surprising theme of the Lord's Supper. We come here because by examining the background and fullness of the Lord's Supper, we learn more about Jesus.

Scripture teaches that taking Communion without a correct understanding can lead to spiritual lethargy or even spiritual death. The opposite is also true—taking the Eucharist with an informed attitude results in spiritual health and vitality.

That's why several years ago I felt God's leading to explore the Lord's Supper in greater detail. As a result, I discovered new aspects of Christ, for the core of the Supper is not the bread and the wine but Jesus Christ.

The purpose of this book is to help everyday people who are seeking a closer walk with God. These were the kind of folks Jesus enjoyed being around. He sometimes laughed with them, sometimes chastised them, and sometimes wept over them. But always he loved them with a love wider and deeper than we can imagine.

I have punctuated this collection of meditations with stories from cultures around the world, which I hope you, as I have, find helpful.

My prayer is that the sacred meal of the ages will draw us nearer to the heart of God and give us fresh perspectives on the Christ we adore.

Let the journey begin.

MEDITATION 1

FOOD FOR THE JOURNEY

And the angel of the Lord came again a second time, and touched him, and said, "Arise and eat, else the journey will be too great for you."

—1 Kings 19:7, RSV

When first-century Roman officials traveled on state business, they took with them their *viaticum*, the necessary provision of food, clothing, and money to see them to their destination. Shortly after AD 100, Christians borrowed the word to describe the Lord's Supper because they saw Jesus, personified in the bread and the cup, as the single most important provision a person could take on life's journey.

Although it may seem we have nothing in common with those first-century Romans, you and I also are on a journey, traveling from the cradle to the grave. Some journeys are longer than others; some filled with more sadness, others with less; and some more troubling or difficult, others less so. But no matter what troubles we endure or privileges we enjoy, all of us encounter life's temptations. Satan, we know, is on the prowl for us—a roaring lion hungering to devour our souls.

I don't know how it is for you, but I grow weary doing battle with the Enemy every day. I sense myself becoming more cynical about politics, more fatalistic toward life, more numbed to the immorality in the world. And sometimes when I am weak, the onslaught of Satan seems furiously strong. At such moments my resolve for battle wilts like a plucked flower on a summer day, much like the exhausted Elijah in 1 Kings 19.

Elijah had engaged in a daylong battle with the prophets of Baal. He exposed them to the people of Israel as false prophets serving a false and powerless god. But under the withering threat of Israel's Queen Jezebel, Elijah ran for his life, hiding in the wilderness like a child cowering in a closet. When he could go no farther, he sat down under a tree and prayed he might die, saying, "I have had enough, LORD." Then he lay down and slept the sleep of the weary and forsaken. That's when an angel of the Lord prepared a meal for Elijah, awakened him, and urged him to eat so the journey would not be greater than his strength.

Have you ever been there? Perhaps you have battled Satan's underlings and by God's grace you won, refusing the temptations they offered. It was difficult, possibly even exhausting. But you won. Then the devil himself showed up, and in your weary condition, you ran. Maybe you even slept Elijah's sleep of despair.

When the journey seems too long and the way too steep for my wearied soul, I yearn for an angel's touch and a nourishing meal from heaven to give me strength to triumph again. That's when I gratefully return to feast at the Lord's Table.

The Jesus represented in the Eucharist and in some spiritual way the Eucharist itself are my *viaticum*, the provision I need for the journey ahead.

On the strength of the angel meal, Elijah traveled "forty days and forty nights to Horeb, the mountain of God." And with this nourishing food of heaven provided by the Lord's Supper, I, too, can make it to the mountain of God.

And so can you.

MEDITATION 2

MORE THAN A MUSEUM OF MEMORIES

The Lord Jesus, on the night he was betrayed, took bread, and when he had given thanks, he broke it and said, "This is my body, which is for you; do this in remembrance of me."
—1 CORINTHIANS 11:23–24

Perhaps you've seen it too. The large oak Communion table at the front of the sanctuary with "Do This in Remembrance of Me" carved on the front—words uttered by our Lord on his blackest night, the night of his struggle with God and his betrayal by man.

If you're anything like me, you know how easily we forget important events such as birthdays and wedding anniversaries. Jesus understood we would forget what he has done for us if we didn't regularly meet with him at the Lord's Table.

When Jesus said, "Do this in remembrance of me," he was urging us to engrave on our memories the blood he shed and the grace he extends. This singular redemptive act, this paying of the debt we could never pay, is the central focus of the gospel. Every other facet of Christianity hangs on this single remarkable event, this hinge point of all human history, this celestial transaction that caught even the angels by surprise.

The Lord's Supper is not like a memorial service for a loved one who has passed away. That person is dead and gone, alive only in our hearts. The Lord's Supper is not that type of memorial because Jesus still lives and interacts with us.

This sacred meal is more than a museum of memories, more than remembering what Jesus accomplished for us once upon a time. It is a thoroughfare into his living presence, a time for encountering him anew. Spending time with him in the Eucharist, recalling his love and sacrifice, continues and deepens our sacred relationship with him.

The broken loaf and poured-out wine are a rich reenactment of Christ's saving sacrifice. When we eat and drink this heavenly meal, our remembrance is awakened. It is no longer a mere cerebral exercise but something that engages our total selves—minds, hearts, spirits, and bodies—making the experience seep into the marrow of our beings.

We keep our remembrance of Jesus alive by honoring this sacred feast in our worship assemblies and by reflecting on his sacrifice with reverence and joy. Through the eating of the bread and the drinking of the wine, we proclaim to the world that God in his gracious love gave his Son to suffer the penalty we deserved. He liberated us so we can again walk with the Father, sinless and forgiven. That's why we share in this sacred meal.

Jesus urged us to participate often in this meal because he knew it would keep our faith alive and well honed, sustaining us in our times of trial.

The Lord's Supper is not an empty religious ritual but a remembrance and celebration of Christ and what he accomplished for us—the event that anchors our souls.

I pray you and I will always hold dear what Christ has done for us in the past. It's essential, too, that we continue to encounter him afresh in the present—especially when we come to the Lord's Table.

MEDITATION 3

A Rose by Any Other Name

Is not the cup of thanksgiving for which we give thanks a participation in the blood of Christ? And is not the bread that we break a participation in the body of Christ?
—1 Corinthians 10:16

What's in a name? A great deal, I imagine, especially if it's your name. In the United States most of us have a first name, a middle name, and a last name. I always knew I was in trouble when my mother called me by both my first and middle names. But in the southern United States, people are often called by both names—like "Betty Sue" or "Jimmy Don"—even when they're not in trouble.

Some nationalities have longer names. Take

Pablo Picasso, for example. His full name consists of twenty words. That's a lot to put on a driver's license.

Churches have used several names for the Lord's Supper. But Shakespeare's line—"What's in a name? That which we call a rose by any other name would smell as sweet"—is equally true of the church's sacred meal. The name does not change either the sweetness or the essence of the Supper.

Many churches since the first century have referred to the church's sacred meal as the Lord's Table or the Lord's Supper because 1 Corinthians 10 and 11 use these very terms to describe it. We honor Christ by using these names because we refer to him as Lord and acknowledge that the Supper and the Table receive their significance from him.

Some churches refer to the Lord's Supper as Communion or Holy Communion. They base this on the King James translation of the Greek word *koinonia* in 1 Corinthians 10:16, which reads, "The cup of blessing which we bless, is it not the communion (*koinonia*) of the blood of Christ?" This name reminds us that we commune with Christ at the Supper. More recent Bible versions translate *koinonia* as "participation" or "sharing" instead of "communion."

Other believers use the name Eucharist, which means "thanksgiving." This is based on the Greek word Paul used in 1 Corinthians 11:24 when he told how at the Last Supper Jesus took bread and gave thanks (*eucharistāsas*) for it. Praising God and thanking him for his gift of salvation through the sacrifice of Christ is an important aspect of the Lord's Supper.

In the past, churches had extensive debates over what happens at the Lord's Supper, but today most churches have reached considerable consensus regarding the sacred meal of the church, though some issues still remain. But the name we attach to it is not as important as focusing on the Lord—his death, burial, and resurrection.

Each name Christians use for the sacred meal of the church contributes a unique flavor of meaning to the Supper. Whatever name you and I use, we must remember the inexpressible, once-for-all sacrifice of Christ.

There is no name on earth as beautiful as his. Nothing excels it or even compares to it. Nothing and no one can stand against it.

So let's give thanks for the relationship we have with the Father because of that sacrifice and commune with Christ as we proclaim his death until he comes again in final victory.

MEDITATION 4

THE LORD'S SUPPER AS SACRAMENT

*When a man makes a vow to the L*ORD *or takes an oath to obligate himself by a pledge, he must not break his word but must do everything he said.*

—NUMBERS 30:2

Perhaps in your church the word *sacrament* is rarely used, and when it is, there is often confusion over its meaning. Many agree, however, that at its simplest, a sacrament is a solemn event established by Christ that reflects his death, burial, and resurrection.

Sacrament was not at first a Christian word, but Christ's followers soon adopted it as their own. It comes from *sacramentum*, an ancient Latin word meaning consecrated or holy. The Romans used it to describe a soldier's sacred oath of allegiance to the emperor. It was required of each soldier upon his enlistment in the military and at various other times during his career.

You can understand, then, why early Christians were quick to make a comparison between the soldiers' oath of allegiance at the beginning of their *military* life and that of believers at their baptism, the beginning of their *spiritual* life. The soldiers repeated their oaths at various times, and the same was true of Christ's disciples through their regular observance of the Lord's Supper.

Both sacraments—baptism and the Lord's Supper—center on Christ's death and resurrection and our response to them. In baptism we pledge our allegiance to Jesus and affirm our sacred duty to serve him. We die to self, are buried with Christ in baptism, and rise out of the water to walk in newness of life. In the Lord's Supper we recall the sacrificial death of our Lord and his promised return. By participating in both sacraments, we relive what God has done for us in Christ and renew our vow, pledging once more our loyalty to the King.

But there is more. God is not silent at the Table, merely observing while we perform our duties. Can you hear him speaking to you through the bread and wine? Can you hear him reminding you once again of what he has done for you, telling you that his Son's death sealed his undying commitment to you?

Yes, at the Table, God reminds you clearly, certainly, and compassionately that he values you as his prized possession. And the best news for those who grew up in families where dad was often absent is that God wants to be your Father—through the best of times and the worst.

It is only then, because of his promises and loving presence at the Table, that you and I can respond with our own pledge, our own sacrament of allegiance, for it is always God who initiates and we who respond. During the sacred moments of Holy Communion, reflect on God's commitment to you, and renew your allegiance to him. God will be praised, and you will be blessed.

MEDITATION 5

The New Passover Lamb

Christ, our Passover lamb, has been sacrificed.
—1 Corinthians 5:7

Have you ever gotten your hopes up only to have someone dash them to the ground like a wrecking ball demolishing a building? If so, you can imagine how the Jewish captives felt when the Lord brought a series of plagues on Egypt. Four times Pharaoh gave in, promising to set them free, but by the next morning he changed his mind and kept them in captivity. One moment hope was alive and well; the next it crumbled into disappointment and broken dreams.

Each time Pharaoh raised their hopes and then cast them into the valley of despair, yo-yoing their emotions from one extreme to the other. Finally the Lord brought a tenth plague upon the Egyptians, a calamity so ghastly that Pharaoh at last relented.

This is how it happened. God commanded each Jewish family to kill a young lamb and apply its blood to the doorframes of their homes. At midnight the Lord passed through the land of Egypt, killing the firstborn son of each home where the doorframes were not marked with blood, "from the firstborn son of Pharaoh … to the firstborn son of the female slave."

Can you imagine the terror that permeated that Egyptian night? The hideous darkness when the firstborn son of every Egyptian and the firstborn male of every animal died, when corpses piled up, and when the cries and wailing of all the Egyptians penetrated every Jewish home?

On that very evening when Egyptians were dying, God gave the Israelite families a visible sign of protection: the lamb's blood on their doorframes. It was God's way of saying, "Amid the death and chaos, take comfort in the security I provide through the blood of the lamb." God consoled his people even while punishing Egypt for her idolatry and rebellion. That night, so full of horror for the Egyptians, filled the Israelites with a fearful awe and thanksgiving for God's mercy.

This rich heritage is the backstory of the crucifixion and the Lord's Supper. You and I know that all those lambs sacrificed in Egypt pointed to the one John the Baptist described as "the Lamb of

God, who takes away the sin of the world!" Jesus is the new Passover Lamb.

During the 1994 Rwandan genocide nearly one million Tutsis perished. My wife and I visited the site where four thousand sought asylum in a church sanctuary designed to seat only five hundred. A mortar shell demolished the front doors, and a mob of machete-wielding butchers worked their way into the helpless crowd.

Blood flowed down the slanted floor toward the front of the sanctuary, rising an inch, then two, and ultimately to six inches in depth. A teenager told his frightened eight-year-old brother, Charles, "Lie down in the blood and do not move. The enemy will think you are dead and will leave you alone." Four thousand innocent people died there in the slaughter that day, and another ten thousand died on the grounds of the sanctuary.

But not Charles. Covered by the blood, he alone was spared.

Is it not the same for us? Covered by the blood of the Lamb, we are saved. The Lord said, "The blood will be a sign for you." The next time you take part in Holy Communion, recall these words as you drink from the cup. And thank Christ for covering you in his precious blood.

MEDITATION 6

AROUND THE WORLD

You will be my witnesses in Jerusalem, and in all Judea and Samaria, and to the ends of the earth.

—ACTS 1:8

The choice of men to whom Jesus entrusted the gospel might surprise you because they were just ordinary folks like you and me—blue-collar working men, fishermen, a tax collector, and a lone seminary graduate who came along later. Yet, empowered by the Holy Spirit, these early disciples took the gospel to the far reaches of the inhabited world.

The Apostle Paul, who was trained in Judaism, established communities of faith throughout Asia Minor and Europe.

But what of the other apostles? Tradition suggests they preached the good news as far away as

India and Persia. Wherever these apostles and their followers went, they spread the news of the one true God.

Imagine you had accompanied me to visit congregations in two of those locations.

You would have seen the elderly Guatemalan Christian of humble circumstances who stood before the rural congregation. Although barefoot, he wore a tattered suit jacket. He held his Bible and read passage after passage, stringing them together in powerful succession as he prepared the congregation to share in the Lord's Supper.

No one else noticed his Bible was upside down, but when I asked him about it after services, he confessed he couldn't read. He had simply memorized the scriptures when he heard others read and then recited the appropriate verses.

I will never forget that spiritual giant though he stood only a little more than five feet tall. Nor will I forget the tears that flowed down the members' cheeks as with pain and wonder they remembered the sacrifice of Christ.

You also would have seen how the sun rose on a Sunday morning over South India, and a Christian woman wrapped the three yards of her best sari around her lithe body. She took the handful of raisins offered by her husband and boiled them in two cups of water, extracting their juices and flavor. When her mixture cooled, she strained out the raisins and placed the liquid on a small table. Beside it she set a *chapati*, a tortilla-like unleavened flatbread.

When the members of the congregation assembled for worship, they gathered around this table to commemorate what the Lord had done for them. Their prayers were in Telegu or one of the other 20 major languages or 720 dialects of India. And our God, who is not limited linguistically, understood their prayers as easily as he does ours.

Nor is our God limited to one region or territory. Wherever his people are found, he is there.

That means you and I are never alone when we take the Eucharist, for God is with us. And as we join hearts with our fellow believers, we form a human chain that encircles the globe. Though we represent a rainbow of ethnicities and speak many languages, we worship the same Father, share in the same meal, and wait for the same Son. The faithful lives of our sisters and brothers around the world enrich us.

Ask our Father to bless these fellow Christians when you next take Communion.

MEDITATION 7

JUST A SYMBOL?

While they were eating, Jesus took bread, and when he had given thanks, he broke it and gave it to his disciples, saying, "Take it; this is my body."

—MARK 14:22

I stood on the sidewalk watching a parade with hundreds of others one windy December day. I was there to honor the grieving spouses and children of fallen American military men and women. When our flag, the symbol of our country, unfurled, I choked up, for Old Glory is more than just a symbol. It embodies for me all that we as a nation hold most dear.

You may have experienced similar moments when the flag passed by and your eyes grew moist, your hand moving, seemingly on its own, to your heart. You stood more erect and perhaps even saluted.

The Lord's Supper is a symbol like that.

But it is also much more.

Some believe the bread and wine are only representations or symbols of Christ's body and blood. The truth is, the bread and the wine are more than simple representations. They *are* the body and blood of Christ, though spiritually rather than physically. And when we eat the bread and drink from the cup, we participate, not in the symbols of the body and blood of Christ, but in Christ's body and blood themselves.

Since the bread and the cup are more than symbols, partaking of them is more than a symbolic act. As we eat and drink these emblems, taking them into our bodies, we seek the Christ behind the bread and the wine, attuning our hearts to him and opening our lives to him once again.

The Lord's Supper is more than a symbol; it is a sign, reminding us of God's covenant with his people, much like the rainbow was for Noah. The Lord said, "Whenever the rainbow appears in the clouds, *I will see it and remember* the everlasting covenant between God and all living creatures." As a sign, it reminded Noah and his descendants of God's salvation through the ark and his promise never to destroy creation by water again. But as a sign, it also had another function—not just reminding Noah and his descendants, but also prompting God to remember his pledge.

And that's how it is with the Lord's Supper. It is a sign reminding you that because of Christ, God has "swept away your offenses like a cloud, your sins like the morning mist." That promise is a balm for your wounds and mine, a cleansing for which our souls have longed, a refreshing respite from Satan's lie that nothing could erase our guilt.

Perhaps it is also a reminder to the Father, a reminder that his Son's blood, symbolically sprinkled on the atonement cover—not the one in the Old Testament temple, but the one in heaven—is sufficient for our redemption. The Supper proclaims God will always remember his covenant with us.

Yes, the Lord's Supper is a symbol and a sign—but oh so much more. When you and I take the Lord's Supper, we are worshipping, interacting anew with the spiritual body and blood of Christ.

What a mystery and what a blessing!

MEDITATION 8

The New Exodus

That you may declare the praises of him who has called you out of darkness into his wonderful light.

—1 Peter 2:9

Sometimes we focus on the wrong thing, putting the emphasis, so to speak, on the wrong syllable. Consider your wedding anniversary, for example. It's easy to get caught up in finding just the right card, buying the desired box of candy, and arranging the perfect date.

But your wedding anniversary should be more than that. It should be remembering the first tentative kiss and the point at which he knew he could not live without you or you without him. It should be recalling your wedding those years ago when you looked into each other's eyes and said, "I do." It should be reliving the bliss of those happy, carefree, and passion-filled years before the children came and reflecting on the passion that has endured through the tumultuous years since.

Your wedding anniversary is a confirmation of your love, a sonnet that celebrates a lifetime of shared memories. It calls for gratitude, honor, and praise. That's what a wedding anniversary is about.

We find a similar linkage in the Lord's Supper. We eat the bread, we drink the wine, and we remember our Lord's sacrificial death. But the Eucharist is much more than that.

The genesis of the Lord's Supper is forever rooted in the Old Testament's first Passover. God's people were captives, fed only enough to stay alive and forced to do hard labor.

It was in that context the Lord said, "Enough!"

He told the Israelites to kill lambs and mark their homes with their blood. Following the deaths of Egypt's firstborn sons and the Passover meal, Moses led the people in a mass exodus from Egyptian bondage.

Jesus built on this event, expanding our understanding by letting us glimpse a new horizon. As the new Passover Lamb, Jesus ushered in a new Exodus, one that liberates us from our enslavement to sin.

Through the Eucharist we recall Israel's escape from physical captivity. More than that, we turn back the clock and take our place beside our spiritual ancestors. We trudge beside them as we leave Egypt and marvel with them as we cross the Red Sea. We eat manna with them and tremble with them as we experience the awesome God of Sinai. And we join with them in a celebratory jig when we set foot at last on Canaan's soil.

Enriched by this experience with our ancestors, you and I can better exult in our own release from the dungeon of spiritual gloom. How wondrous to be rid of Satan's shackles and to walk in the fresh air of God's freedom!

Just as a wedding anniversary comprises more than a card, candy, and a kiss, the Lord's Supper is much more than a piece of unleavened bread, a cup of wine, and somber music. When we take part in this sacred meal of the church, we are identifying with Israel's exodus from Egypt and celebrating our own rescue from Satan's bondage. We rejoice that God has called us out of darkness into the wonderful and liberating light of his presence.

This incredible news of freedom and hope calls for celebrating, praising God, and dancing in the streets!

MEDITATION 9

ALL LOVES EXCELLING

> *I pray that you may have the power to comprehend, with all the saints, what is the breadth and length and height and depth, and to know the love of Christ that surpasses knowledge, so that you may be filled with all the fullness of God.*
> —EPHESIANS 3:18–19, NRSV

I met an elderly Hindu poet in South India who questioned why I had come to tell people about God when India already had millions of gods. I asked if any of his gods had ever loved him or even said they loved him. With some reluctance, a deep breath, and a long sigh, he said, "No."

I replied, "Sir, that is why I have come to India. I want to tell you about the God who loves you."

Like that gentleman, most people around the globe are oblivious to God's love. Nor are they familiar with Jesus, whose love exceeds all understanding.

Paul realized if the Ephesian Christians could grasp even a smattering of Christ's magnificent love, it would equip them to face whatever troubles came their way. So he prayed they would have the ability to understand the breadth, length, height, and depth of that love. Together, these dimensions speak of the vastness of Christ's love.

Oh, that we, too, could begin to grasp the infinite expanse, the immeasurable size of that love.

The Apostle Paul, who penned these words to the Ephesians, experienced Christ's love firsthand. It reached even him, the former persecutor of Christians and destroyer of congregations.

Christ's love also reaches to those the world shuns and the church ignores. It extends to thieves and swindlers, to adulterers and homosexuals, and to drunkards and addicts.

The apostle describes Christians with this kind of a past by saying, "And such were some of you. But you were washed, you were sanctified, you were justified in the name of the Lord Jesus Christ and in the Spirit of our God." That's what Jesus's love does. It changes people's lives.

And the amazing thing about the incredible power of Christ's love is that we who gather around the Lord's Table used to look and act just like those folks. The Lord's Supper shouts that Christ's love for us touched our hearts and transformed our lives though we deserved none of it. Charles Wesley's hymn "Love Divine, All Loves Excelling" says it well: no other love can equal that which Christ has lavished on us.

The beauty of Christ's love is too much for me. It overwhelms me, filling me up and sloshing over the rim of my understanding. It is an incomprehensible love, but to begin to taste it, to experience something of it, satisfies my thirst and refreshes my soul. And it can do the same for you.

Nowhere is Christ's love more evident than at the Lord's Table when we assemble to eat the bread and drink the wine. These sacred emblems are the most extraordinary expressions of Christ's love for us. They are the gospel in tangible form—edible and drinkable. Through the bread and wine, Jesus reminds us that his limitless love continues to cleanse us, continues to wash away our guilt. I stand in awe of that love.

MEDITATION 10

THE MEAL OF SELF-EVALUATION

Whoever eats the bread or drinks the cup of the Lord in an unworthy manner will be guilty of sinning against the body and blood of the Lord. Everyone ought to examine themselves before they eat of the bread and drink from the cup. For those who eat and drink without discerning the body of Christ eat and drink judgment on themselves.
—1 Corinthians 11:27–29

If your life is anything like mine, it is sometimes crowded with the chaos and confusion of our culture. It is so congested, in fact, that it's difficult to find space for reflection and discernment—even at the Table of the Lord.

Can you identify with that?

That's what happened to the church in Corinth. The city's dominant pagan worship style of gluttony and drunkenness invaded the church, masking the sacredness of the Lord's Supper like a solar eclipse obscures the sun. That is why Paul said they were taking the Lord's Supper in a shameful manner.

Eating the sacred meal without reverence and gratitude has consequences. Paul warned that taking the Lord's Supper with such irreverence results in being "guilty of sinning against the body and blood of the Lord." In other words they would bear responsibility for what amounted to nailing his body again to the cross and spilling his blood anew.

Communion is a sacred sharing in Christ's body, which he gave for our redemption. It is a holy encounter with Christ, so holy that God reprimands us when we let the influence of our culture cast a haze over the experience, veiling our view of Christ.

The solution Paul provided for the Corinthians was for all to examine themselves before they ate the bread and drank from the cup. This was to be a rigorous and honest spiritual evaluation. Its purpose was to make sure they approached the Lord's Supper with the right understanding and reverence.

Such an examination could also help you and me.

Some people mistakenly fear they may have committed a sin so appalling that it should keep them from coming to the Lord's Table. But the purpose of examining ourselves is not to dredge up some horrible sin from the past but to spur us to adopt a right attitude and understanding. It is not meant to exclude us *from* the Supper but to prepare our hearts *for* it.

Properly prepared, we realize we come to commune with Christ, not because of our worth but because of our need. A young Haitian girl expressed her fear to a woman missionary—a fear of being unforgivable, "of being too broken" to deserve the grace celebrated in the Lord's Supper.

The missionary responded, "The church is full of broken people …. No one is worthy of the wine and the bread, but that's what makes it so beautiful. He gives us his body because his brokenness can fix ours."

Jesus invites us to come to him with our wounds and our scars, with our burdens and our weariness so he can give us healing and rest. The Lord's Table is the place where, despite our sinfulness, forgiveness is proclaimed and celebrated, where we recall that God, through Christ, extended his grace to make us whole.

That's what evaluating our hearts can reveal. And it's the best news ever.

MEDITATION 11

HIS ALONE

The sacrifices of pagans are offered to demons, not to God, and I do not want you to be participants with demons. You cannot drink the cup of the Lord and the cup of demons too; you cannot have a part in both the Lord's table and the table of demons.
—1 Corinthians 10:20–21

When we approach the Lord's Table, we must come with a commitment to Christ alone. The Corinthians, however, had a flawed concept of the Lord's Supper, believing its regular observation, by itself, was sufficient to protect them from God's punishment, despite their flirting with idols.

Paul urged them to remember the plight of their Jewish ancestors who consumed spiritual food and drink in the wilderness but were still punished for their idolatry. God left their bleached bones scattered in the desert as examples to the Corinthians and future generations.

Some of the Corinthian believers went so far as to accept invitations to the pagan temples and to join in festival meals during which the pagans offered food to their gods. Though these gods did not really exist, Paul knew "behind the nothingness of the idols ... stood demons with real power." These demons, servants of Satan, were intent on diverting allegiance from Jesus to the idols behind which the demons lurked.

Christians sometimes have to make hard decisions about how to interact with culture without forsaking their allegiance to Christ alone. For example, teenage Christians in the Japanese American congregation where I served wondered if they could enter Buddhist temples to attend the funerals of their grandparents. If so, how should they take part?

The standard practice included walking to the front of the auditorium, offering incense to Buddha, pausing at the coffin to bow respectfully to the departed, and then bowing in honor and respect to the family of the deceased.

With help the teenagers concluded they could take part in everything except lighting the incense to Buddha. Just as the early Christians would not worship Caesar, these teens refused to do anything

FOOD FOR THE JOURNEY

that appeased a so-called deity. They wanted to serve Christ alone.

You and I face similar challenges. Facets of our culture, like the sirens of Homer's Greek mythology, beckon us to veer from our course and shipwreck our faith on a rocky shore.

Whom will we serve? That is the big question.

Exodus 21 describes how a Hebrew slave could gain his freedom after serving his master for six years. If, however, the slave was devoted to his master, he could ask to stay. The master then would take him to the doorpost of the home and pierce his ear with an awl. It was a sign that the slave was there to stay, to serve his master permanently.

The hymn "Pierce My Ear" applies this to the Christian who asks God to take him to the doorway and pierce his ear, for he will never give allegiance to another master.

When I take Communion, I know I cannot take part in both the Lord's Table and the table of Satan. I must make a choice. Either I can continue serving Christ or leave his presence to serve another. I choose Christ and him alone.

Anyone for a pierced ear?

MEDITATION 12

THE TABLE OF MERCY

Then he took a cup, and when he had given thanks, he gave it to them, saying, "Drink from it, all of you. This is my blood of the covenant, which is poured out for many for the forgiveness of sins."

—Matthew 26:27–28

Sometimes, perhaps like you, I participate in the Lord's Supper with a measure of trepidation. We know the Supper is an encounter with a holy and righteous Father. He is the God who sometimes has shown his anger in rather dramatic ways: leprosy, blindness, the death of the firstborn—and the list continues.

You and I know that taking Communion is a serious act of worship, one that requires careful spiritual preparation. So as you consider the caliber of your Christian character and the conduct of your Christian life, do you ever fear coming to the Lord's Table? Are you afraid it might result in your being judged unfit, unworthy, perhaps even unlovable? If so, I imagine you have a lot of company.

But the Lord's Supper is not a time for weighing our good points against our sins to see if we are worthy. We are all unworthy sinners in need of grace. Spiritually flogging ourselves because of our shortcomings is not what the Lord had in mind for our table experience.

Such an attitude perverts our understanding of this sacred meal, making it a table of judgment rather than a table of mercy. Even worse, it threatens the heart of the gospel and the meaning of the Eucharist.

Take comfort in knowing that "we have accepted an invitation engraved with the blood of God's Son, and our place at the table is assured." Washed in his blood, we are declared by God as worthy to come to the feast.

I'm reminded of a story I once heard about a missionary who traveled to a remote village in the Eastern Cape region of South Africa. He preached all day Saturday. And before dawn on Sunday morning, his African host awakened him and took him outside to help with a decision.

Still sleepy, the missionary followed his host to a sheep pen where his host told him to select the lamb the women would slaughter and prepare for their lunch later that day. "No one," stated the tribesman, "can be properly welcomed without the shedding of blood."

The same is true for us.

At Communion we drink the cup, remembering that Christ, by shedding his blood, has welcomed us into the kingdom. We come to the Table, therefore, to celebrate, to remember, and to exult in that divine forgiveness, that marvelous and magnificent mercy.

When you next take part in the Lord's Supper, remember that Jesus is waiting for you at the Table, looking for you, hoping for you, as the father did with his prodigal son. When you come, he welcomes you with a kiss on the cheek, a royal robe, and an unimaginable feast.

The Table of the Lord, after all, is not a table of judgment but a table of mercy.

MEDITATION 13

THE MEAL FOR HONORED GUESTS

Then the owner of the house became angry and ordered his servant, "Go out quickly into the streets and alleys of the town and bring in the poor, the crippled, the blind and the lame."

—LUKE 14:21

Do you remember a time when your family and special friends gathered for a meal? Do you recall the laughter, the stories, and the warmth? Grandma's delicious biscuits? Possibly even the child who spilled their milk? Something about meals shared with loved ones draws us together in genuine companionship. In fact, the Latin roots for "companionship" are *com* (with) and *pan* (bread). Breaking bread with others creates a closeness, a connection, a camaraderie.

Maybe that's why Jesus shared so many meals with others. He knew meals were a time of fellowship and acceptance of one's friends and even of strangers who sat around the table.

Consider his meal with Levi, who invited a crowd of fellow tax collectors and other sinners to a banquet he hosted in Jesus's honor. These were the despised outcasts of society. Parents from good families didn't let their children marry these people.

But Jesus went to these broken human beings, to these dregs of society. They were his people of choice. He enjoyed their company, for there was little or no pretense on their part and not much self-righteousness. They were just ordinary folks, wounded, weak, and wandering like sheep without a shepherd. These were the lost ones Jesus came to seek and save. His acceptance of them was genuine, his compassion evident to all.

No wonder they were drawn to him as if by a magnet. Mark says about these men and women, "there were *many* who followed him."

On one occasion when Jesus was eating in the home of a Pharisee, he told a parable about a wealthy man who planned a large banquet. Following Jewish custom, the man issued his invitation weeks ahead so guests could reserve the day. But they didn't know the hour until everything was ready and the servant arrived at their doors.

That's when the excuses arose like a flock of geese taking flight. One said, "I have bought a field and must go to look at it." Another responded, "I have bought five yoke of oxen and I must go and examine them." Still another replied, "I have married a wife and cannot come."

So the master told his servants, "Go quickly to the streets and lanes and bring in the poor and maimed and blind and lame."

Imagine how those who were disenfranchised and despised by society felt walking into that large home, sitting at that bountiful table, eating sumptuous food served on the best dishes, and having servants wait on them! They were no longer the outsiders but the insiders. They were the honored guests at this banquet.

We, too, are the poor and maimed and blind and lame. Nevertheless, God calls us from our brokenness to sit at the Table of the King of kings. Jesus has prepared the banquet. He is the host. And it is no ordinary food we eat, for the bread and the wine are his body and blood. He welcomes us, accepts us, laughs with us, and enjoys being in our presence. We are his kind of people. He loads up our plates, fills our cups, and declares that we are his honored guests.

Oh, the lavish love of God!

MEDITATION 14

THE NEW MOSES

For Moses said, "The Lord your God will raise up for you a prophet like me from among your own people; you must listen to everything he tells you."

—Acts 3:22

Considering Jesus as the new Moses may be an unfamiliar concept for you, as it once was for me. Yet our understanding of Jesus is incomplete unless we see him in that role. After all, that's the identity he revealed at the Last Supper when he said, "This cup is the new covenant in my blood, which is poured out for you." He was mirroring the offering of the blood of bulls at Mount Sinai when Moses said, "This is the blood of the covenant that the LORD has made with you."

There are other parallels between Moses and Jesus. Moses, for example, performed signs and wonders before Pharaoh in Egypt; Jesus performed signs and wonders before the Jewish leaders in Israel.

Moses lifted the bronze snake in the wilderness to preserve life; Jesus said he would be "lifted up" to preserve life.

Pharaoh tried to kill all the male Hebrew babies in Egypt, but Moses evaded death. Herod tried to kill all the male babies in Bethlehem, but Jesus escaped death.

The Israelites were "baptized into Moses in the cloud and in the sea" as they began their life of freedom from Egypt. Believers today are "baptized into Christ" as they begin their lives of freedom from sin.

Moses was a prophet who spoke God's word to the people; Jesus was a prophet who did the same. He said, "For I have not spoken on my own authority; the Father who sent me has himself given me commandment what to say and what to speak."

Moses interceded for the people, and Jesus does the same for those who come to the Father through him.

If we were to summarize the book of Exodus, we could say it is the story of how God saw the people of Israel oppressed in Egyptian slavery and, hearing their cries, sent Moses to deliver them. A summary of the New Testament is remarkably similar. God observed the world enslaved to sin, heard our cries, and sent Jesus to deliver us.

These parallels show us that Jesus is the prophet who supersedes Moses. Moses was the shadow; Jesus is the reality. Moses was the predecessor; Jesus is the Alpha and Omega, the beginning and the end. Unlike the first Moses, Jesus lives forever as the eternal Moses.

Seeing Jesus as the new Moses tells us that God's plan of redemption through the ages has a flawless design. It is not haphazard or ill conceived. We can have confidence in a God like this!

So how does this enrich our time at the Lord's Table?

Understanding Jesus in this new light broadens our concept of who he is and enriches the Supper. This new Moses hears our cries as we suffer under Satan's rule. He frees us with his mighty hand, defeating death's dark dungeon.

Like desert nomads, we depend on him to guide us through the dangers of the wilderness—protecting us from marauders, providing us with nourishment, slaking our desert thirst, and then leading us safely home.

When we take the Eucharist, we remember this new Moses and what he does for us. When we come to the Table, we celebrate that he is our Guide, our Protector, our Sustainer, and our Deliverer.

MEDITATION 15

Bride Prices and Ransoms

For there is one God and one mediator between God and mankind, the man Christ Jesus, who gave himself as a ransom for all people.

—1 Timothy 2:5–6

You may think you aren't worth very much, perhaps like a copper penny in a world of silver dollars. Maybe you believe something is innately wrong with you—that you are clumsy, inept, or unattractive. You may have grown up in a family that majored in negative comments—comments like "Your sister is pretty, but you have a nice personality," as if your sister won the trophy but you got the "I participated" ribbon.

FOOD FOR THE JOURNEY

However it comes, life's cruel treatment leaves scars on our souls. Just ask Mutesi, a young woman in Uganda that a missionary described to me. A deformed leg resulted in a severe limp. Her father's continuous berating left her timid, anxious, and expecting little out of life. He complained he would receive a bride price of only one cow for her, not the standard two or three. When she hobbled by, even the village women whispered to each other and wagged their heads. Rejected and dispirited, Mutesi's self-confidence vanished like a long sigh.

We shouldn't be surprised when the world undervalues us, because it did the same thing to God. When the Lord announced he was severing his role as Israel's protector, he told them, "'If you like, give me my wages, whatever I am worth; but only if you want to.' So they counted out for my wages thirty pieces of silver ... this magnificent sum at which they valued me!"

Did you catch the sarcasm?

More than four centuries later, Judas sold Jesus for the same amount, thirty pieces of silver—the going price for a slave gored by a bull. Thirty pieces of silver for the apple of God's eye! If he had been a woman in Uganda, he might have garnered only a goat or a chicken.

And what about you? What are you worth?

Your condition was desperate, for temptation

had lured you into Satan's prison like a flame drawing a moth to its death. The price for your freedom was a price you could never pay because the price was innocence. And innocent you were not.

Even the cows on a thousand hills would have been an insufficient ransom. So God in his mercy provided his Lamb as a ransom for you, an offering both innocent and pure. His sacrifice gained your freedom and mine, reinstating our innocence and purity before the Father.

And what of Mutesi, the Ugandan woman? A man from a neighboring village fell in love with her despite her defect. He offered her father not the expected bride price of one or two cows, but five cows. Stunned by his love and the price he was willing to pay for her, young Mutesi began holding her head high and acting with greater confidence.

The village women still whispered as she passed by but now with respect. "There goes Mutesi, the five-cow bride!"

The angels, too, are whispering—whispering about you and me. "There they go, the redeemed ones who are neither one-cow brides nor five-cow brides but Lamb-of-God brides."

That is the value Jesus, the Bridegroom, has placed on you. That is your worth. So when you next take the Lord's Supper, lift your head and walk with gratitude and dignity.

MEDITATION 16

THE TOGETHER MEAL

When you come together, it is not the Lord's Supper you eat, for when you are eating, some of you go ahead with your own private suppers. As a result, one person remains hungry and another gets drunk ... So then, my brothers and sisters, when you gather to eat, you should all eat together.
—1 CORINTHIANS 11:20–21, 33

Several California restaurants refused entry to my PhD professor and his wife because of their Asian heritage. And a Texas church turned away my African friend because of the color of his skin. And he was a Nigerian prince!

Prejudice has been a disease in our world since the beginning, and it afflicted ancient Corinth. In the first century Corinth was a prosperous city, but its affluence fostered sharp divisions between the rich and the poor. This cancer spread even to the church, finding expression especially in the Lord's Supper.

Imagine gathering with other believers for a fellowship meal and Communion only to find the wealthier members had begun eating without waiting for you and the other less affluent Christians.

What would you think if you were sitting on one side of the table with little more than a dried fish and a cup of water, while across the table fellow Christians feasted on sumptuous four-course meals? With no hint of sharing? Would you feel unappreciated and disrespected, as though you didn't belong—perhaps even angry?

If so, you can understand what was happening in Corinth. The church was being torn apart by pride and social discrimination.

The Corinthians' thoughtless behavior astonished the Apostle Paul, who responded with strong reprimands. He declared their meetings were doing more harm than good. Their observance of the Lord's Supper was so sinful it wasn't even worthy of being called the Lord's Supper. He wondered if they despised God's church and intentionally were humiliating their fellow believers.

Paul provided two remedies. First, he told them to remember that Jesus gave his flesh and blood for the salvation of the entire world—for the rich and poor alike (1 Corinthians 11:22). He implied Christians should imitate Christ's example by giving themselves to others, regardless of ethnicity, social level, or financial standing. The Lord's Supper was no place to flaunt economic superiority over the poor.

Second, Paul instructed them to eat the Lord's Supper *together*. As with the Old Testament Passover meal, Communion was to be shared with others. It was an occasion for remembering and rejoicing about their shared salvation—a time to celebrate their oneness as God's redeemed people.

Prejudice plagues all of us to some degree until we learn more about each other. When we develop a trust relationship, and learn to love one another for Christ's sake, prejudice dissipates like a morning fog.

There is always room at the Lord's Table for all God's people, regardless of status or color. Our togetherness is like a chorus: all our voices are different, but their diversity results in beautiful music. So whether you are a soprano or an alto, a tenor or bass, come sit beside me. We'll share the *together meal* as we sing to the Lord as one body.

MEDITATION 17

WHEN WILD WINDS BLOW

We are more than conquerors through him who loved us. For I am convinced that neither death nor life, neither angels nor demons, neither the present nor the future, nor any powers, neither height nor depth, nor anything else in all creation, will be able to separate us from the love of God that is in Christ Jesus our Lord.

—ROMANS 8:37–39

Do you sometimes wonder if God has forgotten about you? Or worse, has given up on you? When you look at the problems you face and the troubles in your life, do you feel that God has deserted you? That maybe you are not worthy of his love?

If so, take comfort in knowing the entire Trinity—Father, Son, and Holy Spirit—works continuously on your behalf.

Jesus gave his life for you and is now in the courts of heaven, where he is always interceding on your behalf.

The Holy Spirit, who took up residence within you when you became a Christian, is molding you, transforming your heart and life into the likeness of Christ.

You may still have difficulty praying. The profound thoughts of your heart sometimes are buried too deep for words to convey. So you can only groan and sigh. That's when the Holy Spirit intercedes for you "with groanings too deep for words." The groans are yours, but the thoughts and desires behind the groans are the product of the Holy Spirit working in you. In that sense they are also his groans.

Some concerns are easy to express in prayer because they are surface matters. But others run deeper, like the currents of the sea, and are more difficult to put into words. But even these—the deepest longings of your soul, the most profound yearnings that spring from deep within—he uses to make his powerful intercessions for you.

The Father, who is ruler of all creation, is also on your side. He already gave his Son for you while you were an outsider. Do you think he will back out now after he has adopted you?

Never!

He searches your heart and knows the mind of the Spirit. He hears each of your prayers, perhaps especially those expressed with groans and sighs too deep for words.

Nothing can tear you away from God's fierce embrace or his ferocious love. Neither troubles nor hardships, neither financial reversals nor dangers, nor anything in all creation.

That's how special you are to him.

This is the story of God's profound grace into which you are written as his child. So when the skies darken with storms, when the battles rage and wild winds blow, remember his promise: "Never will I leave you; never will I forsake you."

When next you take the Lord's Supper, praise the Father, Son, and Holy Spirit for never giving up on you—even when you stumble in disobedience or lose your way. The Spirit intercedes for you even when the currents of your heart run too deep for words. Thank him for that.

MEDITATION 18

THE COVENANT MEAL

When Moses had proclaimed every command of the law to all the people, he took the blood of calves, together with water, scarlet wool and branches of hyssop, and sprinkled the scroll and all the people. He said, "This is the blood of the covenant, which God has commanded you to keep."

—HEBREWS 9:19–20

Have you ever wondered why some people disregard their promises? Desecrate their wedding vows? Dishonor their contracts? Whatever happened to "He is as good as his word"?

But here's the good news: God does not break his promises. He declares, "I will not violate my covenant or alter what my lips have uttered."

After God set his people free from Egyptian slavery and gave them the Ten Commandments,

Moses read to them the decrees God had so freshly engraved on the tablets. The people responded, "Everything the LORD has said we will do." So God established a covenant between himself and the Israelites.

Then Moses ordered the people to offer animal sacrifices. He took the blood from those sacrifices and sprinkled it on the people. This was "the blood of the covenant."

Next, Moses and a group of Israel's leaders climbed the mountain, and there they saw the God of Israel and ate and drank before him. This ancient covenant meal and the blood of the covenant were thus inextricably woven together in the most important feast in Israel's history.

The earliest Christians recognized the Lord's Supper as God's covenant meal with them, Christianity's most important feast. God sealed the old covenant with the blood of animals, but the new covenant he sealed with the blood of his only Son, the Lamb of God. This is the rich background behind Jesus's words when he said in Luke 22:20, "This cup is the new covenant in my blood, which is poured out for you."

This new covenant brought reconciliation between God and his people. That is why the title of the 1999 New Testament in the Imbo Ungu language of Papua New Guinea is "The true talk that God said our war is over." That is the significance of what Jesus said when he ushered in the new covenant. The fractured relationship between God and humankind was at last healed by Christ's blood.

As we participate in the Lord's Supper we, like Moses, go up the mountain into the presence of God. We see him—and his holiness and majesty humble us. Then we eat the covenant meal he has prepared.

But a covenant always involves at least two parties. Yahweh will be our God *if* we will be his people. He will guide us and bless us *if* we respond, "Everything the Lord has said we will do."

This is what occurs each time we take part in Communion. We agree once more to be his people as though we were renewing our wedding vows. And Jesus, who is always present and active in the Supper, reassures our hearts that he is forever faithful, keeping his covenant and honoring his commitments.

MEDITATION 19

THE DAY OF ATONEMENT

When Christ came as high priest.... He did not enter by means of the blood of goats and calves; but he entered the Most Holy Place once for all by his own blood, thus obtaining eternal redemption.
—HEBREWS 9:11–12

The sun warmed the crisp morning as the high priest bathed and put on the sacred garments prescribed for the Jewish holy day known as the Day of Atonement. He was nervous today, filled with excitement, awe, and not a little fear.

Excitement because this was not an ordinary day of supervising sacrifices but a special day, occurring only once a year.

Awe because today he was going into the Most Holy Place, or Holy of Holies, the restricted section of the temple where only high priests entered.

Fear because that room contained the ark of the covenant. The lid of the ark and its two golden angels facing each other was God's mercy seat, the atonement cover above which God dwelled in all his holiness. The high priest swallowed several times, knowing it is a fearful thing for a person to come into the presence of the divine.

He first sacrificed a bull on the altar as a sin offering for himself and his household. Then he offered a goat as the sin offering for the people.

After each sacrifice he entered the Most Holy place to sprinkle their blood on the atonement cover.

This ministry of the high priest and the role of the sacrifices he offered are the background for Christ's atoning sacrifice for our sins—an unspeakable gift of grace. But in addition to grace, our atonement required justice. And justice was expensive beyond measure.

This time it required the blood of the perfect Lamb of God.

On crucifixion afternoon when Christ shed his blood and breathed his last, the curtain leading into the Most Holy Place was ripped open, signifying that Jesus, our High Priest, had entered the room and poured his blood on the atonement cover. He made atonement there for you and me and for all who would seek forgiveness and healing from the Father.

The cross was God's altar where he sacrificed his Son, where the Father's love was most evident, and where his need for justice was at last satisfied.

Perhaps your response when first learning of Christ's atoning sacrifice was like mine. I could do nothing but surrender my life to God. Even now, decades later, I am still deeply moved by it. I hope you are as well.

Though the Romans crucified Jesus on Passover rather than the Day of Atonement, his crucifixion ushered in something unexpected, a new Day of Atonement. This was *the* Day of Atonement for which the Jews had been yearning during those bleak centuries when they had only Yom Kippur, a shadowy symbol of this day.

The Lord's Supper reminds us that Christ has made atonement for our sins, removing them "as far as the east is from the west." And the good news is that he continues to remove your sins as you follow him. Every day you walk with Christ is your new Day of Atonement.

Remember this as you take Communion, and lift your praises to the Father of all mercies.

MEDITATION 20

THE MEAL OF RECONCILIATION

Therefore, if you are offering your gift at the altar and there remember that your brother or sister has something against you, leave your gift there in front of the altar. First go and be reconciled to them; then come and offer your gift. Settle matters quickly.
—MATTHEW 5:23–25

The Maasai people of Kenya and Tanzania depend on one another to protect the village cattle from predators and to move the herd to new pastures. When a breach occurs between families, it puts the entire community at risk. To reconcile those families, the villagers rely on an unusual Maasai custom.

They urge the offending and offended families to each prepare a meal. With much encouragement from the other villagers, each family accepts the meal cooked by the other family. They do not refer to this food with the word used for regular food but with a word meaning *holy* food. And when both families eat this meal, forgiveness is offered and received, and a new covenant of unity begins.

Can you imagine how important this kind of reconciliation is for those of us in the family of God? We need one another's encouragement and support as we try to live for him in this world.

Even the best of friendships sometimes fray like an old flag on a windy day. The cause may be as insignificant as a misunderstanding based on a facial expression or tone of voice. Or, more serious, it may be due to a willful sin. But the outcome is the same: hurt feelings, broken relationships, and divisions in the church.

Damaged relationships can devastate a congregation, a village, and a friendship. People take sides. Estrangement occurs, sometimes even among close friends. And we know how deeply that hurts.

Jesus tells us to restore shattered relationships quickly, even to stop worshipping until we go to the offended person and make matters right. The longer we wait, the wider and deeper the gulf becomes, making repentance and forgiveness more difficult.

If the tables are reversed, and someone has wronged you, take the initiative. Talk about the matter with that person, but always kindly, with the goal of restoring harmony.

You may feel alone at church, like an invisible person, perhaps ostracized because of a past conflict with another member. Maybe you hear people talking with one another, but no one is speaking to you.

Like the holy food of the Maasai, a meal of reconciliation awaits, and that meal is the Lord's Supper. We eat holy food, remembering that the Lord offered his body and his blood for all of us, regardless which side of the broken relationship we represent. As we eat, let's seek forgiveness and extend it to others, pursuing the harmony so important to our Lord and so needed by his people today.

Is your relationship with God strained? Does he seem distant and silent? If so, know that his heart aches to walk with you as he did with Adam and Eve in Eden's paradise, even giving his Son to make it possible. Eat the Lord's Supper, the holy meal, with him, confessing whatever has caused the breach, and experience again the joy of reconciliation, of walking once more in harmony with the Father.

MEDITATION 21

THE HIGH COST OF A FREE GIFT

All have sinned and fall short of the glory of God, and all are justified freely by his grace through the redemption that came by Christ Jesus. God presented Christ as a sacrifice of atonement, through the shedding of his blood—to be received by faith.
—ROMANS 3:23–25

Perhaps you are among those who believe the best things in life are free. If so, welcome aboard! I enjoy free things like anyone else, but I'm convinced the finest of all that is free is the gracious forgiveness God bestows on his children.

To be honest though, sometimes I have tried to earn my forgiveness by exercising self-discipline, giving generously to the poor, and being pious—whatever that is. I didn't do well, not well at all. I found only two outcomes to that approach, and perhaps you've discovered the same. If I managed some measure of success, I became a little smug, a little self-righteous, and even somewhat pharisaical.

Or when I kept failing, I became depressed, much like an alcoholic who has fallen off the wagon repeatedly. After a while I wondered, what's the use?

So it's self-righteousness if I gloss over my mistakes or hopelessness if I am honest. These are my constant bedfellows when I try to earn my own salvation.

None of us can merit redemption by our good behavior because we can never be good enough. Everyone sins and stands guilty before the Lord. But the inconceivable wonder of it all is that God declares us forgiven. It's a precious gift he extends to us "freely by his grace." In case we missed it the first time, the Apostle Paul repeats it three chapters later: "The *free* gift of God is eternal life in Christ Jesus our Lord."

While salvation is a free gift for us, it was not free for Christ. He paid the price on a bloody cross. While he hung on that instrument of torture, suspended between heaven and earth, passersby ridiculed him, telling the miracle worker to save himself. They chanted, "Come down from the cross, if you are the Son of God!"

But Jesus did not come down. It would have been easier. It would have been safer. But it would not have been in keeping with his life's purpose. Thank God he did not come down or our sins would still chain us to hopelessness and despair.

Neither was the gift of our redemption free for the Father. The price of our salvation may not have cost *us* anything, but the cost to the Father was horrific. Jesus's cry, "My God, my God, why have you forsaken me?" pierced the Father's heart like a bolt of jagged lightning. The day God sacrificed his Son was the day heaven wept.

The psalmist wrote, "No one can redeem the life of another or give to God a ransom for them— the ransom for a life is costly, no payment is ever enough." Yes, the price of our redemption *is* costly, but thank God his Son's sacrifice is more than sufficient to redeem us.

When I take Communion, I lift my soul in thanksgiving to the Father and the Son for enduring the pain of the high cost of their free gift to me. I am humbled and amazed. And I worship in that spirit when I come to the Table.

MEDITATION 22

THE NEW MANNA

I am the bread of life. Your ancestors ate the manna in the wilderness, yet they died. But here is the bread that comes down from heaven, which anyone may eat and not die. I am the living bread that came down from heaven. Whoever eats this bread will live forever.

—JOHN 6:48–51

When Jesus spoke these words to the people, they would have remembered God's gracious provision of manna that fed their hungry ancestors.

But notice the contrast.

Their ancestors ate the manna provided by God's mercy, but they still died. Jesus, however, is the new manna, the living bread. And whoever eats this new manna will never die. That manna is not his flesh, not his human body, but his very being, his essence.

Jesus's words compel us to recognize him as the spiritual food and drink without which we cannot live. He is our sustainer, our supporter, and the one who nourishes us.

Life without Jesus is a life of shadows and silhouettes, a life of dull grays and blacks. But a life filled with Christ overflows with vibrant reds, greens, and yellows—the vivid hues of purpose, confidence, and hope.

There is a spiritual connection in John 6 between Jesus, the manna, and the Lord's Supper. By eating and drinking at the Lord's Table, we are consuming "the bread of angels," not the old manna that sustained the children of Israel for a day, but the new manna of Christ, who strengthens us forever.

Occasionally recited before the Eucharist are these words: "The Body of our Lord Jesus Christ …. Take and eat this in remembrance that Christ died for thee, and feed on him in thy heart by faith, with thanksgiving."

The Lord's Supper is spiritual food for our souls, nourishing us and confirming our hope. But a meal that is rarely eaten cannot strengthen us forever, any more than one day's supply of manna sufficed for those wandering in the desert. Our nourishment requires consistent feedings, and that is the reason I go to the Lord's Table every week.

A small piece of bread and a sip of wine might seem insignificant. But for Christians this partaking of the body and blood of our Lord is an act of devout worship. It brings us once more into a fresh encounter with Christ, who nourishes, sustains, and strengthens our souls. It is not the physical bread and cup that so empower us, but the spiritual food we receive when we feed on Christ in our hearts by faith.

The crowd clamored for the loaves and fishes but turned away when Jesus declared he was the bread of heaven. Their sin was not that they hungered for physical food but that they no longer hungered for God.

You and I, hopefully, are different. We hunger for the Lord, hunger to be filled with him, hunger to be so brimming over with Christ that our lives reflect his image.

I don't know how it is with you, but I cannot survive spiritually unless I worship regularly at the Lord's Table. Eating the bread and drinking the cup renews my deep hunger and thirst for the Christ, who is "the bread that came down from heaven."

What about you?

MEDITATION 23

OUTSIDE THE CAMP

The high priest carries the blood of animals into the Most Holy Place as a sin offering, but the bodies are burned outside the camp. And so Jesus also suffered outside the city gate to make the people holy through his own blood. Let us, then, go to him outside the camp, bearing the disgrace he bore.

—HEBREWS 13:11–13

I used to think becoming a Christian was the respectable thing to do. Now I know sometimes it is just the opposite.

God's Son poured out his blood on the lonely hill of Golgotha, next to the dumping ground where priests disposed of the carcasses of animals sacrificed in the temple. By dying at this place, Jesus identified himself with a long history of redemptive sacrifices and endured the ridicule of those who watched.

A remarkable woman I met in a village in India was willing to give up her respectability to follow Jesus. I saw in her the fulfillment of Hebrews 13. It is one thing to read about an eagerness to follow Christ; it's another to witness it firsthand.

Villagers gathered on the bank of a small river, pleading unsuccessfully with their Hindu elders for permission to become Christians. No one knew what to do next. Then one of the leading women quietly walked into the water to be baptized into Christ.

For her, following Jesus meant stepping outside the camp of social and cultural norms. It opened her to possible abuse and alienation, but she was willing to suffer his disgrace and share his stigma.

She realized her Hindu environment would never endure eternity. Only the kingdom for which Jesus died would do that. And his kingdom did not abide inside the walls of her traditional religion but outside the camp where he waits.

Jesus calls us to join him there. He does not invite us outside the camp to enjoy the crowd's appreciation but to suffer their denunciation. He does not bid us come to him for commendation but for crucifixion. Only then can we share in his redemptive ministry to bring hope to those still trapped inside the gates.

Unless Christians are a redemptive people, we do not fully reflect the One who died to make us holy. And sometimes that's a bit scary for Christ followers like you and me.

That's why the Lord's Supper is not for the faint of heart. For when we take part in the Supper, we proclaim to the world that this Jesus who suffered outside the gates is the One we emulate. We also proclaim that we, through him, are offering our lives to bring redemption to the world.

The camp, surrounded by its strong walls, seems secure. But such is not the case, for the future is not with the camp. All that is going to burn. The real future is with Christ, who is outside the camp calling us to join him.

When that courageous woman of India stepped into the river for baptism, seventy-six others followed her.

Afterward, she asked me to give her a Christian name. I said to her, "Your name is Mary, because, like Jesus's earthly mother, you were willing to suffer dishonor and reproach to bring Christ into the world of your village."

What about you and me? Are we ready to declare our commitment to Christ through the Lord's Supper? If so, let's go to him outside the camp.

Mary is already there.

MEDITATION 24

SETTLING FOR LESS

Jesus said to them, "Very truly I tell you, unless you eat the flesh of the Son of Man and drink his blood, you have no life in you.... Just as the living Father sent me and I live because of the Father, so the one who feeds on me will live because of me."
—JOHN 6:53, 57

A violent earthquake struck Guatemala while my family and I were living there. It shook the nation like a bulldog shakes a rag doll, collapsing buildings, creating landslides, and killing more than 23,000 people. One-fifth of the population was suddenly homeless. Two days later I was distributing food to the survivors when I approached a young barefoot boy, still numb from the tragedy, his fists clamped around handfuls of pebbles. I offered him a sack of bread, but he wouldn't let go of the gravel to accept the gift. He was settling for pebbles instead of bread.

Have you ever done that? Settled for less when more was available?

Perhaps you were afraid of failure, so you froze with fear.

Maybe you were comfortable where you were, your heart deadened to the dangers of the status quo. Or you may have settled for less because you were numb to life's possibilities.

Sometimes we respond in the same way to our Father in heaven, settling for less when he wants to bless us with much more.

Jesus faced a crowd composed of people like the Guatemalan boy. After he miraculously fed the five thousand, a throng pursued him to get more of the free bread. They wanted only the physical bread even though he offered spiritual food that could have satisfied their deepest hunger.

I pried open the small boy's fingers until the pebbles fell to the ground, and replaced them with the bread he needed. Unlike me, Jesus doesn't pry open our fingers. He never compels us to accept the nourishment he offers. He only invites and pleads, never forces.

But the crowd refused Jesus's invitation and was deaf to his urgings. They settled for pebbles instead of riches, for less rather than more.

Sometimes it's that way when we take the Lord's Supper. Too often you and I give our attention to passing the Communion tray, shushing our children, or preparing for the offering. We occupy ourselves with the trivial instead of the profound, settling for scraps when Jesus has prepared a banquet.

Jesus declares he is the bread of life and unless we feast on him, we will never truly live. He promises that if you and I hunger for him the way drowning sailors gasp for air, we will enjoy incomparable riches for eternity.

Though Jesus's words from John 6 are not directly about the Lord's Supper, they have implications for how we take Communion. He yearns for us to focus on taking him into our lives, drinking him into our souls, absorbing him so he is in every cell of our spiritual beings—we in him, and he in us.

Let's not settle for less.

MEDITATION 25

Knowing Christ

That I may know him and the power of his resurrection, and may share his sufferings, becoming like him in his death, that if possible I may attain the resurrection from the dead.

—Philippians 3:10–11, RSV

Knowing Christ was Paul's chief objective, his ardent passion, the hunger of his soul. What he desired was not a list of facts *about* Christ, not more theories or theologies about the Savior. He wanted to know the person of Christ, Christ *himself*. He wanted to experience him, not just casually, but deeply.

Spanish has two words for "to know." One is *saber*, meaning to know about. The other is *conocer*, meaning to experience. You can *saber* the city of Madrid by reading a book about it. But you cannot *conocer* Madrid until you stroll along its Gran Vía and tap your foot to live flamenco music. That's the meaning of the word Paul uses here for knowing Christ—not just reading about him, but experiencing him.

Sometimes I struggle with knowing Christ as intimately as Paul desired. Sometimes life closes in, its pace becomes frantic, and I get distracted.

Is it the same with you?

You may recall a time when your walk with Christ was vibrant and full, but then it faded like an old photograph left too long in the sun. You may not remember the precise moment your relationship with him began to decline, but one morning you awoke and realized life was empty, and Christ seemed distant.

Maybe, like me, you have listened to sermons about Christ. But they weren't enough because you hunger for something more personal, more intimate. The same was true for Paul. He had heard the Savior's voice on the Damascus road and the message from Ananias, yet he yearned to know Christ more deeply.

Paul believed that knowing Christ meant sharing his suffering. He believed that when Christians endure trials for their faith, they somehow share in Christ's adversity, absorbing the affliction he would have experienced if he were still here.

Paul also recognized that knowing Christ meant experiencing "the power of his resurrection." Devout as Paul was, he hungered for a life more consecrated, more fully conformed to Christ's will. But he realized he could not attain this on his own; only the power evident in Christ's resurrection could bring the desired changes.

He knew this power was not a thing of the past as if it were confined to some spiritual museum. This power was available to him and continues to be an available force to transform our lives.

To know Christ as Paul knew him likely means experiencing Christ on a deeper level than ever before. That's why the Lord's Supper is so essential for us.

At the Table we encounter Christ's suffering and death anew, and are reminded again of the power of his resurrection. This draws us ever closer into communion with our blessed Lord.

When we take Communion, we declare to the Lord and to one another that Christ is the One for whom we long. He is our supreme objective, our ardent passion, the One for whom our soul hungers. Consider this the next time you take the Lord's Supper.

MEDITATION 26

THE TABLE OF TEARS

No one could distinguish the sound of the shouts of joy from the sound of weeping, because the people made so much noise.
—Ezra 3:13

Early missionaries to Africa learned Christians there referred to the Lord's Supper as the Table of Tears. The name makes sense when we consider the tears of Jesus in the garden. They were tears of loneliness, for he had no one to watch and pray with him. They were also tears for the isolation awaiting him on the cross when even his Father would abandon him.

But Jesus no longer weeps alone. His followers often mingle their tears with his, especially at the Lord's Supper.

You and I may try to overlook the severity of our sins by rationalizing they are not as offensive as those of others. We may excuse ourselves by confessing we are only human. But when we are confronted with the reality of what sin did—what *our* sin did—that it crucified the Son of God, we are jolted by sin's offensiveness.

Sometimes the Eucharist reminds us of this dreadful consequence. And that realization often pierces our hearts like a volley of arrows. That's when tears leak from our eyes because of our many sins. Some tears are solitary droplets of remorse; others are rivers of grief coursing down our faces. Still others remain hidden from view inside our weeping hearts.

These tears may not occur every time we take the Supper, but they appear often enough for us to refer to Communion as the Table of Tears.

This is the land of remorse, where there are tears of sorrow for sins perhaps committed in our distant past or for transgressions we committed only yesterday. They are iniquities we know broke our Father's heart and crucified his Son.

Have you been to that land?

Maybe you are there now. Your sins may weigh heavily on your shoulders like giant hands of lead. You may cry out with David as I have, pleading, "Have mercy on me, O God, according to your unfailing love; according to your great compassion blot out my transgressions. Wash away all my iniquity and cleanse me from my sin."

The Lord delights in this kind of sincere prayer and honest tears. And he responds as he did to Hezekiah: "I have heard your prayer and seen your tears; I will heal you."

But tears of sorrow are not the only tears shed during the Lord's Supper. Tears of joy are also present because the abundance of our sins is dwarfed by the magnitude of God's forgiveness. This forgiveness, this gift of tender love, causes our hearts to melt before God's magnificent mercy.

Jesus loves to change our tears of sorrow into tears of joy. Speaking of his coming death, he said, "You will grieve, but your grief will turn to joy." I have shed both kinds of tears at the Lord's Table. Perhaps you have done the same. When we next meet at the Table of Tears, I'll loan you my handkerchief.

MEDITATION 27

THE MEAL
THAT NOURISHES

For those who eat and drink without discerning the body of Christ eat and drink judgment on themselves. That is why many among you are weak and sick, and a number of you have fallen asleep.
—1 CORINTHIANS 11:29–30

Your spiritual life might be going nowhere, like a sailboat on a windless night. Just sitting there, bobbing up and down, but making no progress. Your walk with the Lord once may have been exhilarating, your prayer time precious, and your days filled with inexpressible peace.

But now you're in the spiritual doldrums.
> Rocking back and forth.
>> Dead in the water.

That, and worse, happened to the Christians in Corinth. They once possessed a vital and obedient faith, their hearts filled with gratitude for God's transforming power. But then spiritual lethargy crept in—and sin soon followed. They began eating and drinking the Lord's Supper with little or no thought of its spiritual significance.

Their thoughtless and irreverent observance at the Table led to two devastating outcomes. First, they ate and drank judgment upon themselves. Second, the meal no longer provided spiritual nourishment. And that led to weakness, sickness, and even death.

While some people understand this to be a physical punishment, most see this as having spiritual consequences. If we eat the Lord's Supper irreverently, we forfeit the spiritual nourishment we otherwise would have received. We become spiritually weak and sick. Some may even die spiritually.

The bread and wine of the Lord's Supper speak to us of the spiritual food for which we yearn—Christ himself, not the literal bread of Communion, but the bread of heaven. William Williams describes our deep hunger:

> Bread of heaven,
> Feed me till I want no more.

The Supper by itself neither wards off spiritual ills nor provides spiritual nourishment. But it draws us to Christ and he is the One who heals our spiritual sickness and feeds our souls.

The Corinthians were in danger because their flippant observation of the Lord's Supper was alienating them from Christ, the Bread of heaven. Without him, their spiritual lives were languishing and death was waiting around the corner.

Am I like the Corinthians? Are you?

When we recognize our spiritual lives, like the sailboat, might be stuck in a windless night, we pray, even at the Table, "Bread of heaven, Bread of heaven, feed me till I want no more."

The wonder of it all is that when we regularly participate in this sacred event with spiritual and reverent hearts, the Lord himself feeds our spirits and nourishes our souls. He does this with the very food we must have in order to live, and that food is himself.

Then perhaps once again the fresh wind of the Holy Spirit will fill our sails.

MEDITATION 28

The Meal of Haste

This is how you are to eat it: with your cloak tucked into your belt, your sandals on your feet and your staff in your hand. Eat it in haste; it is the LORD's Passover.

—Exodus 12:11

Have you experienced a crisis that demanded urgency? Perhaps your house was on fire, and you grabbed your phone and punched in the emergency number. Or you found your young child floating facedown in the swimming pool. With fear crashing over you like an icy wave, you sprang into action, clearing their mouth and administering CPR.

There was an emergency in Egypt every bit as frightening. After generations of being in slavery, the Jewish people learned their exodus was imminent. But first God's people had to eat a meal that would shape Israel forever and forge the heart of Christianity for all time.

The Jewish captives were to eat that meal, the first Passover, in haste, ready for a rapid departure. The Lord gave them three directives. First, he told them to gather the ends of their long robes and cinch them around their waists with a belt. With their loins girded, they would be ready for the long march.

Second, God instructed them to eat this Passover meal with their sandals fastened securely to their feet, their walking shoes laced and ready for travel.

Finally, he told them to eat standing up with a staff in their hands. The staff was their trekking pole and sometimes also their weapon for protection. The wise traveler never embarked on a journey without one.

With food in their stomachs, belts cinched, sandals laced, and staff in hand, the Jews were ready for a quick escape.

There was a reason for this haste. Pharaoh had often promised to release the Jews, but each time he had reneged. Now, devastated by the tenth plague, he once more gave permission, so they needed to leave quickly before he changed his mind again. Even though they hurried, the recalcitrant Pharaoh nearly overtook them at the Red Sea.

Considering the Lord's Supper as a meal of haste

is important for our spiritual growth. Life is short, and no one knows when it will end. Our days and nights are too valuable to waste.

Though you and I have experienced much of the Spirit's transforming power, we see areas of our lives still under Egypt's influence. We need to bring those spheres under God's liberating control. And we need to do it quickly.

If we have tasted the sweetness of forgiveness, it's time to leave captivity in the rearview mirror. Once we drink his blood and eat his body, we cannot stay in Egypt any longer. Lingering means continued imprisonment.

So where are you on your spiritual pilgrimage? Are you satisfied with your walk with Christ, or do you still desire to go deeper into the Lord? Smash the chains that hinder you, and snap the bonds that bind you to a mediocre faith.

Whether our time is long or short, let's take immediate steps to be ready for the rest of our journey. Daylight is burning, and it's time for action.

When I take the Lord's Supper, I often pray I will approach my journey to heaven's Promised Land with a sense of urgency and haste.

Why don't you grab your trekking poles and join me?

MEDITATION 29

THE MEAL OF PURITY

For Christ, our Passover lamb, has been sacrificed. Therefore let us keep the Festival, not with the old bread leavened with malice and wickedness, but with the unleavened bread of sincerity and truth.
—1 CORINTHIANS 5:7–8

Are you aware that both Passover and the Old Testament Feast of Unleavened Bread form the backdrop for the Lord's Supper? Both feasts celebrated the Jews' rescue from bondage and their exodus from Egypt.

Not only are they similar, but their celebrations overlap.

Because the two feasts are so intertwined, God's Word considers them two feasts in one. Luke noted, "Now the *Festival of Unleavened Bread*, called the *Passover*, was approaching....

Then came the day of *Unleavened Bread* on which the *Passover* lamb had to be sacrificed." Passover, therefore, was part of the weeklong Festival of Unleavened Bread.

Both feasts required Jews to remove every trace of yeast, or leaven, from their homes. The Lord warned, "For seven days no yeast is to be found in your houses. And anyone, whether foreigner or native-born, who eats anything with yeast in it must be cut off from the community of Israel."

That's why Jewish families ransacked their houses, looking in every pot and every corner of their homes to make sure they had removed all traces of leaven. The tiniest particle, even a spore of it floating in the air, could contaminate a batch of dough.

Leaven came to signify evil, so Jesus warned, "Beware of the leaven of the Pharisees and Sadducees." And Paul urged us to live not with the old leaven of "malice and wickedness, but with the unleavened bread of sincerity and truth." God wants us to be pure in our thoughts and actions, uncontaminated by evil.

While Passover was a meal of haste, the Feast of Unleavened Bread was a meal of purity and dependence on the Lord, and so is the Lord's Supper. Paul instructed us to cleanse our hearts of any impure attitudes before we eat the unleavened bread of the Eucharist.

But spiritual purity is fragile since leaven can so easily infiltrate our hearts. That's why we need to examine our lives regularly to discover if any of our traits or habits offer an opening for Satan. Even a small measure of evil can, like a fungus, infect our whole being. A single sin repeated becomes a habit. Then if unchecked, it becomes an addiction that dominates our lives.

So let's throw out the old leaven by taking off our old selves of malice and evil, as if they were stained and tattered coats. Let's embrace a fresh start with the new leaven of sincerity and truth, asking Christ to clothe us with our new identities—identities fashioned by righteousness and holiness.

And here is the beautiful news of the gospel. When you and I do our best to ferret out every particle of leaven, we can confidently trust God's grace for anything we have overlooked.

As you take the unleavened bread of the Lord's Supper, pray with me for your life and mine to reflect Christ's purity as we journey together toward our heavenly home.

MEDITATION 30

THE ONE-LOAF MEAL

Because there is one loaf, we, who are many, are one body, for we all share the one loaf.

—1 CORINTHIANS 10:17

I recall once worshipping with men and women from various cultures and nationalities. We hailed from Africa, Asia, and Europe. We came from North America, Latin America, and other parts of the world. What impressed me was that despite our differences in ethnicity, education, and economics, we were all one in Christ.

We were like grains of wheat God had gathered from the far reaches of the earth and ground into flour so each individual seed shared some of its identity with the others. Like grain that is gathered, ground, and finally baked into a single loaf, we worshipped the Lord together.

Paul said the one loaf of the Lord's Supper is symbolic of our unity in Christ.

Sometimes partaking of the Communion meal is for you a private matter, a cherished moment between you and the Lord. A time to reflect on the depths of his love and what that means for you. And, considering that love, to determine how then you should live. The same is true for me.

But a single seed of wheat does not make a loaf. Nor does a solitary Christian make up the body of Christ. That's why the Lord's Supper is a communal meal, a meal we share with fellow Christians. This hallowed meal is a symbol of our unity.

We cannot base this unity on shallow sentimentality. Nor can we base it on our agreeing on every iota of doctrine or practice. Instead, our unity results from our being born anew into the family of God. Any other basis ends in division.

A miracle of sorts occurs here, for God takes you and me—two individuals who once were our own lord and master—and forms us into a single body with Christ as the head. Once we were selfish and proud. But now as we experience the transformation of the Holy Spirit, we are learning, however imperfectly, to serve one another in love and to honor one another above ourselves.

We meet our brothers and sisters at the Table of the Lord, and we eat the loaf in joyful harmony. We also meet Christ at the Table, and if our hearts are right, he brings us closer to one another.

The Didache, an important Christian document from the second century, reflects on our coming together to take the one loaf of Communion. It offers this prayer: "As this broken bread was scattered upon the mountains, but was brought together and became one, so let thy Church be gathered together from the ends of the earth into thy kingdom, for thine is the glory and the power through Jesus Christ for ever."

May our Father grant us a passion for unity so we may all be one, just as he and the Son are one. And may our experience of feeding on the one loaf so enrich us that we praise him with one voice, one heart, one soul, and one mind.

MEDITATION 31

Thanksgiving and Celebration

Ten men who had leprosy met him. They stood at a distance and called out in a loud voice, "Jesus, Master, have pity on us!" When he saw them, he said, "Go, show yourselves to the priests." And as they went, they were cleansed. One of them, when he saw he was healed, came back, praising God in a loud voice. He threw himself at Jesus's feet and thanked him.

—Luke 17:12–16

You would have been shocked, as I was, if you had seen Vahini, a woman I met at a leper colony in India. Her nose was missing, leaving only a jagged hole where it had been. Several of her fingers were also absent, and her eyes were leaden, testifying that hope had long ago been extinguished. Leprosy, a terrible, disfiguring disease, scars its victims for life.

You and I also are afflicted with leprosy, but a far more crippling strain than leprosy of the body. Ours is sin, a leprosy of the soul that disfigures and devours our inner selves until all that remains is a raw hole in the center of our beings. And it scars us not just for this life but also for the one to come.

But Jesus heals our leprosy and restores our hope. Then, like the cured leper of Luke 17, we throw ourselves at Jesus's feet, thanking him and praising God.

That's what the Lord's Supper is about—giving thanks and praising God. That's the meaning of the word *Eucharist*, which many Christians since the second century have used for the Supper.

Because of Jesus's example, prayers of thanksgiving have always introduced the bread and the cup. Such prayers have varied in wording, depending on the time and place. But central to those prayers are gratitude and praise—gratitude for Christ's sacrifice and praise for "the riches of God's grace that he lavished on us." What can we do but respond with thankful hearts and arms raised in praise when we experience such grace? We can no more silence our praise than songbirds in the spring can hush their singing.

Even if we were gifted with the tongues of angels and the vocabulary of the most educated, we could never exhaust the praises our God deserves. Nevertheless, he is pleased even when with halting lips we simply say, "Thank you, Father."

Such honest gratitude is the hallmark of the Eucharist. It opens our hearts to the God who delights in the world he created and rejoices over those who are grateful.

When you next take the Lord's Supper, remember Jesus is the Great Physician. He has healed your leprosy and filled the empty place in the center of your soul. He poured his love and forgiveness into that cavity, resurrecting your hope and making you whole. Bow before him in thanksgiving and awe, for he is your redeemer, your healer, and the One who restores your soul.

MEDITATION 32

THE MOUNTAINS OF FEAR AND JOY

But you have come to Mount Zion, to the city of the living God, the heavenly Jerusalem. You have come to thousands upon thousands of angels in joyful assembly, to the church of the firstborn, whose names are written in heaven. You have come to God, the Judge of all, to the spirits of the righteous made perfect, to Jesus the mediator of a new covenant.

—HEBREWS 12:22–24

Is your Christian experience defined by dread and doom? Or is it characterized by gratitude and grace? The writer of Hebrews 12 contrasts two mountains: a mountain of fear and a mountain of joy. Which will you choose?

First he describes the mountain of fear. Try putting yourself in the sandals of those standing near the foot of Mount Sinai when God issued the Ten Commandments. Flashes of lightning streak across the threatening sky, followed by deafening peals of thunder. The hairs on the back of your neck stand at full attention as darkness drapes the mountain. A paralyzing fear grips you and your companions in its sharp claws. A trumpet from heaven blasts a warning to come no further, for the majestic holiness of God is so dangerous that no animal or sin-stained person can touch the mountain or they will die.

Then the terrifying voice of God thunders his commandments, and, like Moses, you tremble with fear. God's mandates are so stringent that you want to flee from this mountain and get away from God's voice. You beg him, "Please be silent!"

Maybe that's the mountain you have been living beside, a religion dominated by fear, "darkness, gloom and storm." But God is not inviting you to that mountain.

Instead, he calls you to the mountain of joy described in Hebrews 12:22–24. This is Mount Zion, where Jesus gave his life for us, where he ushered in the new covenant, and where he established the Lord's Supper.

Let the Lord transport you to this mountain of joy so you can catch a glimpse of your life in Christ. What is it like as you stroll through that garden city of God? What is it like as his forgiveness envelops you and cleanses you, leaving you unburdened by guilt? What is it like to experience his healing balm wash over the wounds of your heart? Tell me what it's like to hear choirs of angels and get caught up in their joyful worship, to rejoice with them, laugh with them, and praise God with them.

On this mountain you come into the very presence of the Almighty, but God has banished your fear, so you come with rejoicing and gladness. By the gift of Christ's death for you, the Father has transformed the terror of Sinai into this mountain of joy. His grace has recreated you to delight in his love, mercy, and healing touch.

Relish these blessings when you stand on this mountain taking the Lord's Supper. Remember, it was the body and blood of our Lord Jesus Christ that made these mercies a reality.

MEDITATION 33

THE NEW CREATION

Therefore, if any one is in Christ, he is a new creation; the old has passed away, behold, the new has come.
—2 CORINTHIANS 5:17, RSV

My son and I hung our hammocks in the open air on an old stern-wheel riverboat and then journeyed some eight hundred miles down the Amazon River from Colombia.

A short distance seaward from Manaus, Brazil, we witnessed what Brazilians call the "Wedding of the Waters." Here the inky Rio Negro joins the sandy brown Upper Amazon, and the two flow side by swirling side for miles without mixing. Their two colors stay clearly distinguishable until at last they form a new creation—a river of a different and blended color.

Your life is like those two rivers, and so is mine. In the past we lived as captives of sin. But at some point our lives intersected with the divine, and we cried out with King David, "Create in me a clean heart, O God, and renew a steadfast spirit within me." Then Christ entered our story, and at that confluence everything changed—sometimes dramatically and sometimes less so, depending on how immersed we were in the dark side of life.

When we died to our old patterns and began following the Lord, we were transformed into a new people, a new creation. God does not, however, accomplish our spiritual transformation overnight. We are works in progress. Like the waters of the Rio Negro and the brown Upper Amazon, parts of our old lives coexist side by side with our new lives.

There are still old habits and fruitless ways of thinking that we need to change. It's a neverending task because we are not yet fully formed in the image of Christ. But God, who never sleeps, continues creating in us a new river, a new life, a new identity.

An important instrument he uses in this process is the Lord's Supper. Just as in the Wedding of the Waters, at the Supper two streams meet; heaven and earth intersect. At Communion our earthly selves meet the Christ of heaven and interact with him. And that interaction, repeated over time, changes us. Our hearts join his as he wrestles in Gethsemane and writhes under the heavy lashes of Roman whips. We agonize with him when he endures the cross, and we rejoice with him when he abandons the tomb for his resurrected life and his place at the right hand of the Father.

Scripture says at that moment Jesus became the *firstfruits* of those who have died. That means others, including you and me, will follow with our own resurrections. In the Lord's Supper we already taste that future. We know that when we leave the grave, our journey, our transformation into the image of Christ, will be complete in all its fullness. The two rivers of heaven and earth, of eternity and time, will at last wed to form our eternal future.

And what a future that will be!

But even now as you eat the bread and drink the cup, thank the Father for being the God who came to earth. Praise him for intersecting with your life, for cleansing and shaping you for heaven. Ask him to continue working on you until his life is fully formed in you. As your life courses downriver with Christ—roiling, flowing, mixing—may his mercy, love, and healing continue working on your heart until the two of you become one.

MEDITATION 34

HEALING THE SHAME

How much more, then, will the blood of Christ, who through the eternal Spirit offered himself unblemished to God, cleanse our consciences from acts that lead to death, so that we may serve the living God!
—Hebrews 9:14

Brian and his wife, Megan, visited their friends one wintry night, and Brian uncharacteristically had one too many drinks. He insisted on driving home but didn't see the icy patch in time. The car spun off the highway, slammed into a tree, and killed his wife.

Brian knows God has forgiven him. But the shame persists, eroding his self-worth like a rainstorm battering a barren hillside.

Shame tells its distorted version of his story, whispering to Brian that he is a worthless drunk and murderer, undeserving of pity or forgiveness. Its relentless barrage twists Brian into a labyrinth of pain and despair.

Does shame whisper in your ear its false versions of your story as it does into mine? Shame is Satan's tool to shackle us to the dishonor of our past.

We find God's answer for our shame in an unlikely place—the story of Adam and Eve. Before they sinned, they were naked and unashamed. But after they sinned, shame surfaced like an ugly wart on their souls. First, it prompted them to sew rough garments of fig leaves to cover themselves. Then it drove them to hide in the bushes.

That's what shame does: embarrasses us, compels us to cover up, and drives us into hiding. Like Adam and Eve, we try to conceal ourselves even from God.

God showed up, despite their guilt and shame, and called, "Where are you?" When Adam said they hid because they were afraid and ashamed, God asked, "What have you done?" Adam confessed they had eaten the forbidden fruit.

What did God do? Turn his back on them? Forsake them? No. He did what we would never expect. He made better clothes for them, clothes of animal skins to further cover their shame.

And he does the same for us, not with animal skins, but with the blood of Christ. It's the perfect covering because no one who believes in Christ will ever "be put to shame."

God does more than cover our shame. He restores our honor. Some cultures believe in honor killings. When a family member brings shame to the family, they kill that person to remove the family's shame and restore its honor.

But when we brought shame on the family of God, he did not kill us. Instead, he sacrificed his own Son to remove the shame and restore the honor. Not just the family's honor, but also our personal honor.

He does this not by disowning us but by adopting us into his own family and seating us with his Son in the heavenly places. We are children of the King and there is no higher honor than that.

If shame is crushing your spirit, remember that God can shepherd you through the snarl of your shame and provide relief and healing in Christ. That's what Brian is learning.

When you take Communion, thank the Father for covering your shame with the blood of his Son and for restoring your lost honor. Remember he declared, "I broke the bars of your yoke and enabled you to walk with heads held high."

MEDITATION 35

GRACE REIGNS!

Where sin increased, grace increased all the more, so that, just as sin reigned in death, so also grace might reign through righteousness to bring eternal life through Jesus Christ our Lord.

—ROMANS 5:20–21

I used to assume that when I sinned, God withheld his grace. Now I know just the opposite is true. And I hope you have discovered it too.

Regardless of what you've done, no matter how sin has reigned in your life, you can find forgiveness in the Christ of Holy Communion.

Maybe you believe your sin doesn't merit God's forgiveness. You're right; it doesn't. But that's the beauty of grace. It gives you what you don't deserve but what you desire in the depths of your soul.

The more I focus on my sins, the heavier my

burden becomes. That weight can crush any hope I might have of pleasing the Father. A more balanced view, a healthier approach, takes into account not just my sinfulness but also God's abounding grace.

As difficult as it is to imagine, when you sin, God lavishes even more grace upon you, not less. And his grace reigns in you, not because of your perfection, but because of Christ's perfection and your need.

This doesn't mean we should take our sins lightly. But neither should we allow our lapses to dictate who we are in Christ. Such an attitude offends our Father, insinuating his grace is insufficient for our salvation.

When Paul wrote the extraordinary words "grace increased" in Romans 5:20, he did so by adding the prefix *hyper* to the verb. So when sin increased, grace *hyper*increased or "increased all the more." Our Father does not dispense his grace like a miser who gives only a few coins to the destitute. Instead he pours into our lives his "abundant provision of grace."

Notice what God's extravagant grace accomplishes in our lives: we are saved "by grace," "justified freely by his grace," and God our Father "loved us and by his grace gave us eternal encouragement and good hope." The whole sweep of

Scripture shouts that God's eternal purpose is the triumphant reign of his grace!

The wonder is, imperfect as we are, God has declared us righteous because of Christ. We still stumble, but when we do, "we have an advocate with the Father—Jesus Christ, the Righteous One. He is the atoning sacrifice for our sins."

When you eat the bread of Communion and drink from its cup, remember that no sin is so terrible that God cannot forgive. He does not withhold his grace because of your sin. Instead, he lavishes his grace upon you until it abounds and overflows, until it covers your sins and cleanses your soul like a gentle kiss from heaven.

That's the legacy of the cross and the empty tomb. And that's the message of the Lord's Supper: grace undeserved and freely given. Grace abundant and healing. Grace abounding to eternal hope and grace bigger than any sin or mistake.

MEDITATION 36

THE MESSIANIC BANQUET

I say to you that many will come from the east and the west, and will take their places at the feast with Abraham, Isaac and Jacob in the kingdom of heaven.

—MATTHEW 8:11

Have you ever found it difficult to get yourself in the right mood for taking part in the Lord's Supper? Some people believe they should always adopt a somber state of sorrow for Christ's sufferings. If that's where you are, let me suggest that's not the only acceptable state of mind.

The Lord's Supper looks not only to the crucifixion and death of Christ but also to the future, a future marked by a joyous victory celebration. Christians call that celebration the Messianic banquet.

Jesus referred to this banquet when he established the Lord's Supper, saying, "I tell you, I will not drink from this fruit of the vine from now on until that day when I drink it new with you in my Father's kingdom." After the Supper he added, "I confer on you a kingdom, just as my Father conferred one on me, so that you may eat and drink at my table in my kingdom."

This feast will occur when everything has been placed beneath our Lord's feet and he has handed over the kingdom to his Father. We will know Jesus then as King of kings and Lord of lords. The banquet will signify the kingdom of God has invaded Satan's world, set the captives free, and defeated death—Satan's last weapon of mass destruction.

The Messianic banquet will be a victory party because Christ's triumph over Satan will be a cause for celebration! That celebration will draw crowds of faithful believers from the far reaches of the earth. And we will sit with them at the Messiah's banquet, rejoicing, fist-bumping, and praising.

The Lord's Supper, like the Messianic banquet, is a victory celebration. The victorious outcome of the cosmic battle between God and Satan is guaranteed. Christ is risen, and our hearts are full of joy.

Even now every time we partake of the Lord's Supper, Jesus is participating with us and pointing us, leading us, to the breathtaking victory celebration that awaits.

FOOD for the JOURNEY

Some Christians unfortunately have missed the joy of the Lord, finding it easier to put on a dour face than to laugh and celebrate. They take after King David's wife Michal, who despised her husband for what she considered his less-than-royal behavior when he danced in the streets to celebrate the overdue arrival of the ark of God.

But David was right. It was a time for rejoicing and dancing. While I am not suggesting we dance around the Lord's Table, I am saying Holy Communion is at least worthy of joyful celebration.

If that surprises you, consider the response when the people of Israel returned to Jerusalem after seventy years of captivity and could finally observe the Passover again. Scripture says, "For seven days they celebrated with joy the Festival of Unleavened Bread, because the LORD had filled them with joy." Did you hear that? Joy and celebration are gifts of God.

The Lord's Supper is a celebration of hope, for the Lord God Almighty reigns. Let us be grateful and full of joy!

MEDITATION 37

THE LORD'S FERVENT DESIRE

When the hour came, Jesus and his apostles reclined at the table. And he said to them, "I have eagerly desired to eat this Passover with you before I suffer."
—LUKE 22:14–15

Have you ever wondered how best to get ready for the Lord's Supper? Maybe it's as simple as looking into the heart of Jesus and seeing how earnestly he wants to commune with us.

The Lord understood that suffering and death waited for him. He knew he must go from the Last Supper to the cross. He realized betrayal and abandonment would occur before the next sunrise. He was aware he would experience a lonely death and burial in a borrowed tomb. And he realized it was our sin that caused it all.

Knowing all that, Jesus still said, "I have eagerly desired to eat this Passover with you." Not just desired to eat with the disciples, but longingly so, fervently so. At that meal he revealed his heart to them, defined his life's purpose, and established the Lord's Supper.

Jesus sits enthroned at the right hand of the Father. Yet even now he yearns to eat with his people, to share a meal with us in warm companionship. And that meal of bread and wine is himself: "Come drink, this is my blood of the new covenant. Come eat, this is my body given for you."

Is this not an indescribable blessing?

Jesus sees our struggles. He understands the battles we've fought, both those from which we emerged as victors and those when we waved the white flag of surrender. He has seen us stumble and fall, and he has seen us get up from the mess we've made and continue our journey limping toward him. He sees it all. And at the Table his love provides exactly what you and I need to satisfy the hunger of our souls.

Are you overwhelmed, as I am, by our Lord's eagerness to share the Supper with us, when it was our sins that drove in the nails?

A Catholic priest visited a madrasa, a religious training school for Muslims in his native India. At the madrasa he and the students ate together off the same plate.

One student told him, "We eat together like this at home. It is the mark of being together as one family. You are a member of our family. It is a sign of our trust for one another."

Another Muslim student said, "When we eat from the same plate, our love for one another is deepened."

Perhaps that's why Jesus wants to share the Supper with us. Eating together signifies we are his people, his family. And sharing the bread and the wine with him enriches our love for him and his love for us.

When we next meet Jesus at the Table, let's remember his strong desire to eat with us, and let's relish his longing to enjoy the kind of closeness that exists between dear friends. I want to bask in his presence, and I'm sure you feel the same.

MEDITATION 38

WAITING:
THE TIME BETWEEN

Do not leave Jerusalem, but wait for the gift my Father promised, which you have heard me speak about. For John baptized with water, but in a few days you will be baptized with the Holy Spirit.

—ACTS 1:4–5

One Christmas season during my childhood I wanted to open a present early, thinking it might be the Red Ryder BB gun for which I had been hoping. Christmas was days away, and waiting was not high on my list.

Maybe you are experiencing a time of waiting, perhaps even a significant time, and you are languishing. They have taken the biopsy, but you must wait for the results. Your company is downsizing, people are being laid off, and you're wondering if you will be next. Or worse, your child in the military is missing in action, and you must wait in suspense.

Waiting is agonizing when so much hangs on the outcome. Benign or malignant? Employed or jobless? A happy reunion or a devastating loss?

What do you do with that interminable space between first hearing about the problem and finally learning its outcome?

Here's what the disciples likely did when Jesus told them to reenter Jerusalem and wait for the power of the Holy Spirit. While they waited, they recalled his teachings, remembered his miracles, relived the seasons of his companionship, and raised their hands in prayer.

It must have been difficult to wait during the ten days from Christ's ascension to Pentecost. Imagine the burden of keeping the great secret of the ascension to themselves for that long.

Yet there was a profound purpose in God's delay. The waiting was educational. The power of prayer on their knees forged them into a stronger band of disciples. Their hearts changed. Their resolve strengthened. And their doubts converted into certainties. All while they waited.

Waiting is a great teacher and shaper of persons.

Christians have waited since the ascension for the fulfillment of another promise, one every bit as important as that for which the early disciples waited. We await Christ's return. The angels declared to the apostles, "This same Jesus, who has been taken from you into heaven, will come back in the same way you have seen him go into heaven." That's an assurance that makes our souls sing. We have the promise but must still wait for its fulfillment.

Waiting is a gift too valuable to be squandered, and only we can decide how it will be spent. So how do we use the time between Christ's ascension and his return?

I'll share one practice that helps me. I take the Lord's Supper every Sunday, the day of the Lord's resurrection, because it keeps me focused on Christ and his return. It assures me he has not abandoned me. Nor has he abandoned you.

He is present even now in the sacred meal. And through the bread and wine, he lifts our spirits and heartens us while we serve him in the here and now. Waiting for Christ's return is sometimes like a slow-moving stream reluctant to reach the sea. But the day will come when he does return. Then the hope we have nourished during these years of waiting will be swallowed by an eternity in his glorious presence.

This is the magnificent truth we celebrate during Communion.

MEDITATION 39

THE COSMIC BATTLE

Then war broke out in heaven. Michael and his angels fought against the dragon, and the dragon and his angels fought back.
—REVELATION 12:7

When Orson Welles decided in 1938 to broadcast a dramatization of a Martian invasion of Earth, he had no inkling of the panic it would cause. One million radio listeners of the presentation of *War of the Worlds* thought a real Martian invasion was underway. Cars jammed New Jersey highways, trying to escape. People begged police for masks to protect them from Martian toxic gas. And one woman, thinking all hope was lost, ran into an Indianapolis church during services screaming, "It's the end of the world! Go home and prepare to die!" But even a real Martian incursion, if such were possible, would pale when compared to the cosmic battle waged in heaven—a battle pitting Satan and his demons against God and his angels. This is the ultimate war of the worlds!

The theme of cosmic warfare is introduced at the beginning of the Bible when the Serpent lures Adam and Eve away from the Lord. And it concludes when God destroys Satan and his demon army in the last book of the Bible.

Between these bookends an ongoing battle takes place. The venomous Serpent invaded Cain's jealous heart, prompting him to murder his brother. Satan persuaded King Herod to try to kill the young Jesus. But even though Herod slaughtered all the young boys in Bethlehem and its vicinity, Jesus and his family escaped to Egypt.

After failing in that attempt, Satan tried to persuade the adult Jesus into worshipping and serving him. That plot also proved futile, so the Devil redoubled his efforts to destroy the Lord. Eventually he turned the hearts of the Jewish leaders against Jesus, and they convinced the Romans to crucify him.

Scoffers scoffed. Guards gambled. Mary wept. And the prince of demons rejoiced.

Can you imagine how Satan must have relished what he thought was his delightful victory over God? The relief he must have felt, knowing that at last the Savior was dead and his redemptive mission scuttled?

Caught unaware, Satan discovered too late that by shedding Jesus's blood, he ironically served God's purpose to bring salvation and hope to the world. And by that act the Serpent, who tried to kill the King, was himself vanquished!

But on that fateful Friday afternoon, darkness and gloom hung shroud-like over the dead body of Jesus, and the disciples scattered like smoke in the wind.

Have you experienced times when the hope within you died and life appeared to be at a dead end? Times when your dreams shattered and healing seemed impossible?

When struggles besiege me and my hope grows dim, I recall that every Friday is followed by a Resurrection Sunday. No matter how dire the situation, how dreary the prospects, how dismal the circumstances, Christ still reigns as Victor.

When you and I take the Lord's Supper, we celebrate this triumph over Satan. And we proclaim—not just to ourselves, but to the principalities and powers, to the angels and demons, and even to Satan himself—that God has already won the victory in the only war of the worlds that counts.

MEDITATION 40

THIS IS HOLY GROUND

"Do not come any closer," God said. "Take off your sandals, for the place where you are standing is holy ground."
—Exodus 3:5

What turns an ordinary place into a sacred space? Perhaps the best answer is found in Moses's experience while shepherding sheep in the Midian desert. He noticed a burning bush, but the flames were not consuming it. Curious, he drew near to inspect the strange sight. The Lord spoke from the bush, saying, "Take off your sandals, for the place where you are standing is holy ground."

It was not holy because of its location. It was not holy because Moses was there. It was holy because the God of the Ages was present, intersecting with Moses's life.

That's it, isn't it? Ordinary places become holy when God is present.

God always knows where you are whether you're in Egypt or in your own private Midian. He'll come to you there, just as he showed up for Moses at the burning bush. That place will be holy ground for you. His words to you will be the same words he spoke to Moses: "Take off your sandals, for the place where you are standing is holy ground."

Joshua heard the same words from the commander of the Lord's angel armies: "Take off your sandals, for the place where you are standing is holy."

Jacob had a similar experience. He saw the Lord in a dream, and when he awoke, he realized, "Surely the LORD is in this place, and I was not aware of it." Filled with wonder he declared, "How awesome is this place!" Then with reverence and fear he worshipped and made a vow of commitment to God.

Moses, Joshua, and Jacob were all standing on holy ground.

What about you? What about me?

When God intersects our lives, are we standing on holy ground without realizing it? Do we travel so fast through life, riveting our eyes habitually on our smartphones, that we fail to see the burning bushes God has put in our paths? And thus fail to encounter God?

Perhaps Christ gave us the Lord's Supper so we would stop our frantic pace, silence the noise bouncing inside our heads, and draw near to God. It is holy ground because Jesus, our Immanuel, is the divine host, serving us spiritual food through the bread and wine.

What, then, should be our response? I cannot answer for you, but I try, though imperfectly, to imitate Moses and Joshua. Mentally I remove my shoes, for I realize at the Lord's Supper I am standing on holy ground.

Like Jacob, I try to recognize that God is present. I focus on the magnitude of that holy encounter so I am filled with a fearsome wonder that prompts me to bow in worship.

Before you and I receive the Lord's Supper, let's pause and take a deep breath. Then try to absorb the reality that each time we meet Christ at the Table, God pierces the thin membrane between heaven and earth to remind us of the forgiveness and healing he provides through his Son.

How awesome and holy is that moment!

Maybe that's why many refer to the Lord's Supper as *Holy* Communion.

MEDITATION 41

BETRAYAL AT THE TABLE

And as they were at table eating, Jesus said, "Truly, I say to you, one of you will betray me, one who is eating with me." They began to be sorrowful, and to say to him one after another, "Is it I?" He said to them, "It is one of the twelve, one who is dipping bread into the dish with me."
—MARK 14:18–20, RSV

The response of the apostles that solemn night when Jesus revealed one of them would betray him must have encouraged our Lord. Shocked, their spirits immediately deflated with sadness, like balloons pierced by a dagger. Then each one courageously asked, "Is it I, Lord?" The thought that they might prove disloyal horrified them.

Judas, the one of whom Jesus was speaking, asked the same question: "Surely you don't mean me, Rabbi?" But his hollow question was meant to deceive, for Satan had already entered his heart as if the door was wide open and the welcome mat was out. He had made a pact with the Jewish authorities to deliver Jesus into their hands. All that remained was for him to signal when they might take Jesus prisoner without fearing the crowds.

He still could have backed out. But when night, dark as doom, shadowed the city, Judas left to continue his diabolical scheme.

Though that same night Peter would deny the Lord three times, his was a momentary lapse. He tearfully repented, and afterward he became a stalwart leader among the disciples. But Judas was different. He had long been a deceiver and a thief, and those traits led to this night of infamous betrayal.

His example shows we can walk with Jesus for years and not be transformed. If we are not vigilant, the devil can enter our hearts as deftly as he did with Judas.

When you meet Jesus at the Lord's Table, do you sometimes ask, as I do, "Is it I, Lord?" I may have struggled with issues of faith and practice since last meeting him there. And when I take part in the Lord's Supper, my mind is sometimes as cluttered as a hoarder's closet. Nor does my attitude always foster a meaningful communion with Christ. Yet I still muddle through.

"Is it I, Lord? Surely it is not, is it?"

Yes, it is I. Raising this question, however, can be a healthy experience if it leads me to examine myself before eating the bread and drinking the cup. And the same is true for you.

God wants genuine disciples, not plastic pretenders. Honest people. People who see their frailties but have good hearts. They can be corporate executives, blue-collar workers, or day laborers as long as they are humble followers who have the right disposition.

Like the apostles, how well we perform isn't necessarily what pleases Christ the most. Our attitude, our heartfelt contrition—that is most pleasing. For "the sacrifice acceptable to God is a broken spirit; a broken and contrite heart, O God, thou wilt not despise."

These words encourage our souls, enabling us to become, with Peter, loyal disciples of the Christ we adore.

The next time you take Communion, ask with me, "Is it I, Lord?"

MEDITATION 42

GREAT EXPECTATIONS

For whenever you eat this bread and drink this cup, you proclaim the Lord's death until he comes.

—1 CORINTHIANS 11:26

Jesus was crucified, his body buried, and the tomb sealed, leaving his apostles dazed and bewildered. Darkness descended on their hearts like a shroud, wrapping around their souls, suffocating the hope they once held so dear.

Have you ever encountered a similar occurrence, when despair eclipsed your hope, leaving only emptiness and pain in its wake? If so, you can identify with these disciples.

When demons come in the night to steal our future, we are left confused, our lives a jumble like a pile of tangled twine.

The disciples were numb with grief, their hopes

in tatters, and their lives a maze of pain through which they had to find their way. Then another shock shook their world.

The grave was empty!

Even after all Jesus's teachings, the disciples were not expecting the resurrection. When the women faced the empty tomb, they thought someone had stolen the Lord's body. And the men were as mystified as the women, still not understanding that Jesus *had* to rise from the dead.

Although it was good news, the resurrection brought even more instability and confusion. What did Jesus's resurrection mean for their lives? What were they to do now?

To clear their heads enough to make sense of it all, Peter and some of the other apostles decided to go fishing, distancing themselves from the problem until the numbness wore off.

They knew Jewish leaders were responsible for the crucifixion and that Roman soldiers sealed the tomb. But the resurrection taught them something new.

God is a grave robber!

Instead of wailing, they worshipped. Instead of moaning, they marveled. Hope replaced the disciples' despair, turning their night into day. Jesus was alive!

Not just alive, but we know today he is sitting at

the right hand of the Father. And he is coming again to claim his bride, to take possession of those who hunger and thirst for him.

And we, his bride, wait for him, breathless with hope for his return. That is why we can eat the Lord's Supper with enormous anticipation—an anticipation renewed each time we come together for the Communion, proclaiming "the Lord's death until he comes."

We know there is value for us in taking the Lord's Supper, but have you considered there is also value for the Father? The very act of taking Communion declares to fellow Christians and the world at large that our Savior died, was raised, and is coming again. This delights the Father and brings glory to his name.

The grave could not keep God's Son wrapped in its dark embrace. Death could not be the final word for him, and neither is it the last word for us. Christ was victorious, and in him we, too, are victors.

The resurrected King is resurrecting us, breathing new life into the dead persons we once were. He is shaping our hearts, transforming our souls, and preparing us to meet him on his return.

Yes, he is coming again!

That is the *great expectation* we celebrate at the Communion table each week.

MEDITATION 43

For the Joy Set before Him

For the joy set before him he endured the cross, scorning its shame, and sat down at the right hand of the throne of God.
—Hebrews 12:2

See Jesus weeping alone in Gethsemane's painful night as the shadow of the cross falls heavily upon him. Notice how a cloak of sadness descends, filling him with despair and dread as he considers the full weight of being humanity's Sin Bearer. Listen as he confides to his disciples, "My soul is overwhelmed with sorrow to the point of death."

There is no evidence anywhere else in Scripture that Jesus shared his pain with the disciples. But the agony he experienced that night drove him to seek the companionship and understanding of his closest friends. All of us, even Jesus, need friendship and sympathy when the ebony wings of night overwhelm us.

That bleak evening in Gethsemane, Jesus struggled with his fears and wrestled with God. He knew the Father expected him to sacrifice his life as the perfect Lamb, and that thought filled him with dread. So as you and I might do in difficult circumstances, he prayed for God to change his will. Listen to his loud cries as he pleaded, "My Father, if it is possible, let this cup pass from me."

But it was there he also prayed, "Yet not my will, but yours be done," and won the victory. Jesus fought the decisive battle for our souls not on the cross, but in the garden.

From the moment he surrendered his will and rose from his praying, no temptation could sway him from his purpose, no satanic argument could deter him from his course.

But what motivated Jesus to embrace his crucifixion?

Incredibly, Jesus endured the cross "for the joy set before him." It was the joy of his imminent homecoming and his reunion with the Father. It was the triumphant joy of completing God's purpose in the universe and the expectant joy for the renewal of the glory he had before the world began.

The joy set before him was also the joy of

knowing what his suffering and death would accomplish for us. They would rescue us from death's unrelenting grip, revive our hope, and reserve an eternal seat at his side in the heavenly realms. This was the joy God set before him, and it was this joy that kept Jesus headed unwaveringly to the cross.

My heart delights in knowing that Christ has removed my sin and reconciled me to the Father. Knowing that he willingly and joyfully endured humiliation and pain to obtain my salvation overwhelms me with joy.

Perhaps we should approach Holy Communion with joy for what Christ so joyfully did for us. His victory in the garden, after all, was also our victory. What he accomplished on the cross was, by grace, our eternal triumph.

Christ's joy is waiting for us when we meet him at the Table. May our souls sing with gratitude for the freedom he has purchased for us on the cross. And may the fact that Jesus did this because of his unmitigated joy knit our hearts ever closer to his.

MEDITATION 44

SCORNING THE SHAME

For the joy set before him he endured the cross, scorning its shame, and sat down at the right hand of the throne of God.
—HEBREWS 12:2

Shame is never a pleasant experience. That's why you and I do our best to avoid it at all costs. Even so, sometimes shame turns up uninvited, like a thief in the night, stealing our self-respect and our dignity.

What about you? Do you recall an experience with unwarranted shame? Maybe it was a lie about you that someone shared on social media, or maybe it was the secret you shared in confidence with a trusted friend who later told others.

You're not alone because Jesus also experienced unjust shame.

For him it began with the charade of a trial before religious leaders whose hearts were far from

God. Mere men, pompous and self-righteous, had the audacity to stand in judgment of the Almighty Son of God.

Shame continued when soldiers spit in his face, beat him, and then paraded the condemned and bloody Jesus as he half-walked, half-stumbled to his execution.

Finally came the crucifixion itself, the most degrading form of capital punishment in the Roman Empire. Reserved for slaves and the vilest criminals, crucifixion was an execution perfected by Rome, perfected not only to inflict unspeakable pain on their victims but also to humiliate them. Prisoners were stripped and hung on crosses along the main roads leading into a city. Dying slowly in agony, they were put on public display so passersby could mock them and shake their heads in derision.

Dying the death of a criminal was degrading for Jesus, but there was a shame far worse. It was the shame of receiving the curse of God.

How was he able to bear this shame?

He endured it by scorning it, by showing contempt for it, and by despising it. In other words, he considered the shame of crucifixion insignificant when compared to the joy of redeeming you and me. His perseverance resulted in being exalted to the Father's right hand, where he now intercedes on our behalf.

But scorning the shame of the cross does not mean that the shame was insignificant. Weighed down with a sorrow so deep it nearly crushed him, his forlorn heart cried from the cross, "My God, my God, why have you forsaken me?"

Psalm 69:19–21 further describes the high cost of scorn Jesus paid:

> You know how I am scorned, disgraced and shamed;
>   all my enemies are before you.
> Scorn has broken my heart
>   and has left me helpless;
> I looked for sympathy, but there was none,
>   for comforters, but I found none.
> They put gall in my food
>   and gave me vinegar for my thirst.

When we take the Lord's Supper, we often consider Christ's physical suffering. But we likely have not thought seriously about the shame Jesus endured for us. I plan to correct that the next time I take Communion, and I invite you to do the same.

MEDITATION 45

THE KISS OF DEATH

Now the betrayer had arranged a signal with them: "The one I kiss is the man; arrest him."

Going at once to Jesus, Judas said, "Greetings, Rabbi!" and kissed him. Jesus replied, "Do what you came for, friend." Then the men stepped forward, seized Jesus and arrested him.

—MATTHEW 26:48–50

Did you know the phrase "kiss of death" likely originated with the treasonous kiss of Judas? It came to mean a mortal blow that spells defeat for something or someone. And that was Satan's intention for Judas's kiss—a mortal blow to God's Messiah.

The irony is that Jesus knew Judas was a thief and a betrayer even before he chose him to be an apostle. No one forced Judas to do anything against his will, yet he remained spiritually aloof with no desire to repent.

His weakness was the love of money, especially other people's money. In fact, his first recorded words in Scripture show his covetous spirit. When Martha's sister, Mary, poured a pint of expensive perfume on Jesus's feet, Judas objected. He growled, "Why wasn't this perfume sold and the money given to the poor? It was worth a year's wages."

But Judas didn't care about the poor. He had sticky fingers, and as treasurer for the group, he often helped himself to the money bag.

When Jesus told him to leave the woman alone, Judas refused to soften his heart. Instead, after being deprived of the proceeds from the sale of Mary's perfume, he seems to have immediately hatched another plan to feed his greed. He approached the chief priests and asked, "What are you willing to give me if I deliver him over to you?" These are his second recorded words in Scripture.

Greed, like the grave, is insatiable.

The Jewish leaders gave him thirty pieces of silver. From then on he watched for an opportunity to betray Jesus.

At the Last Supper, while Jesus and the Twelve were eating, Jesus told Judas, "What you are about to do, do quickly." So Judas left the upper room, closing the door forever on his fellow apostles and the Son of God. He gained what he most valued and lost what he most needed.

Jesus and the other apostles then walked to Gethsemane, where Jesus prayed. Not long afterward, Judas arrived, leading a detachment of soldiers and a mob armed with swords and clubs. He went at once to Jesus and kissed his cheek.

Jesus responded, "Do what you came for, friend."

Those were the last words Judas ever heard from Jesus. Not "Well done, good and faithful servant." Only "Do your infamous deed."

Those are words I never want Jesus to utter to me. And I'm sure you feel the same.

Satan doesn't always confront us head-on. He comes first with a whisper in the night, with a suggestion here and a question there. Like an expert angler, he uses one lure after another, tempting and enticing. And once he gets his hooks into us, he moves in, inhabiting our hearts until we are willing to do the unthinkable.

That is one of the reasons the Lord's Supper is so important to me. It strengthens my faith, renews my resolve, and centers my life in Christ so I can resist Satan's pull to join Judas in betraying my Lord. And it can do the same for you.

MEDITATION 46

THE LORD'S SUPPER AS SACRIFICE

Through Jesus, therefore, let us continually offer to God a sacrifice of praise—the fruit of lips that openly profess his name. And do not forget to do good and to share with others, for with such sacrifices God is pleased.

—HEBREWS 13:15–16

Picture yourself worshipping in Jerusalem during Old Testament times. Early one morning you lead an unblemished ox to the priests as a peace offering. The priests kill the ox and place its fat and entrails on the altar as a burnt offering, the smoke ascending before the Lord as a pleasant aroma.

That Old Testament peace offering, also known as a fellowship offering, was distinct from most sacrifices. First, it was a sacrifice not to seek God's favor but to thank him for blessings already received.

Second, the peace offering was unique because the worshippers ate the meat of the sacrificed animal. After the priests placed the fat and inner parts on the altar, they cooked the rest of the animal. After they took a portion for themselves, they gave the rest to the worshippers, who shared it with family and friends in a joyous feast.

We know Christ's once-for-all sacrifice for our redemption replaced the Old Testament sacrificial system. Yet even Christians are told to present certain sacrifices to God. The passage in Hebrews just cited encourages us to offer continual sacrifices of praise to the Father. Those sacrifices do not atone for our sins, but like the peace offering, they praise God for the grace we already have received.

The writer of Hebrews also instructs us to offer sacrifices of good deeds and to share our resources with the poor, both of which please our Lord. Additionally, Paul charges us to present our bodies daily as living sacrifices to honor God.

But how can taking part in the Lord's Supper be a sacrifice we offer to God?

We cannot offer God the body and blood of Jesus, as some believe. He gave them to us once for all. *He* is the giver; *we* are the receivers. We can, however, offer to God at the Lord's Table our prayers of gratitude for the sacrifice of Jesus, whose body and blood are dramatically symbolized by the broken bread and poured-out wine.

We can lay these expressions of gratitude before the Lord as if we were placing them on the temple's altar. They are our sacrifice of praise to the Father. The Lord's Supper can also be a time of sacrifice if, while taking it, we offer ourselves to God "as those who have been brought from death to life."

The act of taking Communion, the prayers you and I offer, and the thoughts upon which we meditate during the sacred meal honor God. But our prayers and thanksgiving, no matter how earnestly given, cannot compare to the sacrifice Christ made for us on the cross. His sacrifice, not ours, is supreme, and it is that sacrifice we celebrate in the Lord's Supper.

MEDITATION 47

Under His Wings

Whoever dwells in the shelter of the Most High will rest in the shadow of the Almighty ....
He will cover you with his feathers, and under his wings you will find refuge; his faithfulness will be your shield and rampart.
—Psalm 91:1, 4

When life beats up on us and we are weary, when the doctor confirms the diagnosis and we are afraid, when we have been abused and we are hurting—it is then we long for a place of refuge, a shelter from the storm.

The writer of Psalm 91 understood our yearning for a sanctuary, a place of rest. And he found it in the "shelter of the Most High" and in "the shadow of the Almighty."

He continued, "He will cover you with his feathers, and under his wings you will find refuge."

The feathers refer to the pinion feathers, those on the outermost edges of the wings. God stretches his entire wings, even to their furthest tips, to protect his children. The psalmist speaks wondrous words of comfort to people like you and me who are desperate for a safe place, a place for rest and healing.

When we read this psalm, we might think God protects us from every calamity of life—from "the terror of night" to "the plague that destroys at midday" and everything in between.

Does that mean no one who seeks protection under God's wings will be a victim of abuse or slander? Our experience tells us such is not the case. Earthquakes and tornadoes take their toll on Christians and unbelievers alike. Cancer still reaches its insidious tendrils under those wings to claim another victim.

So what does Psalm 91 mean?

It means no *eternal evil* can hurt us. Nothing that happens—whether disease, distress, or death—can do us eternal harm. Even the agonizing death of Christ resulted in a blessing for all of us. And Christians around the world celebrate it regularly in the Lord's Supper.

Sickness, injury, bereavement, and suffering may leave us battered and bewildered, but they do not touch our eternal safety. We are under his wings.

Those splendid wings have never failed, never faltered, and never folded.

The devil and his demon army pummel those wings with all their strength to get to us. Satan and his minions have been relentless at this since the dawn of time but without success. And when hell's fury is spent, God's sheltering wings will still be there, providing protection and sanctuary through the storm.

At the Lord's Supper I recall the wings of God that protect me daily from Satan's attacks. God's wings, in my mind, take on the shape of the cross. And in the shadow of that cross, I find my safe place, my sanctuary for healing, and my haven for rest. I thank Christ for the lashing he absorbed for my healing and for the hammer blows that spiked his body to the cross for my salvation.

I love being under these wings of God, safe in the shadow of the Almighty, for here I experience his warmth and tenderness. Here, nestled close to him in this Holy of Holies, I feel the beat of his heart against my ear and discern something of the depths of his love.

Do you hear it too?

MEDITATION 48

CROSSING ON DRY LAND

The priests who carried the ark of the covenant of the LORD stopped in the middle of the Jordan and stood on dry ground, while all Israel passed by until the whole nation had completed the crossing on dry ground.
—JOSHUA 3:17

I looked with mouth agape at fall colors stunning in their brilliance—waterfalls of oranges, yellows, and deep reds cascading lazily down the Canadian mountainside into concentrated pools of color. Surrounded by this beauty, I prayed, "Lord, help me never to take this for granted."

We may wonder how anyone could get used to such wondrous sights. Yet some people who see it year after year do become blind to the majesty of it all.

The same is true of the Lord's Supper. Simple repetition sometimes insulates us from the beauties attached to this sacred feast. To change this, we must pierce the haze enveloping our minds and focus with razor sharpness on the blessings found in this holy meal.

It may help if we look at God's story of redemption as pictured in three miracles. First, there was the miracle at the Red Sea. When the Israelites fled Egyptian captivity, God parted the water so they could cross to the wilderness on dry ground.

The Israelites composed songs praising the power and grace of the Lord who is majestic in holiness and awesome in glory. These hymns helped Israel remember their miraculous and gracious rescue from Egypt.

Forty years later when God's people were about to enter the Promised Land of Canaan, the Jordan River stopped them dead in their tracks. The normally gentle river was at flood stage, making it a raging torrent impossible to cross. But God worked a second miracle by stopping the flow of the Jordan, enabling the people to cross on dry ground.

The Lord told these settlers to remove twelve boulders from the riverbed and stack them on Canaan's shore. When their children later asked the meaning of this pillar of rocks, their parents recounted how the Lord interceded so they could cross into this land on dry ground. This pillar of stones helped them avoid taking their land for granted.

God also performed a third miracle—the miracle of Bethlehem. God's Son took on human flesh and offered his life as atonement for our sins. God parts the waters with his grace so we can cross from the wilderness of our sins to the Promised Land of forgiveness. If it were not for the Lord, we surely would drown in the swirling sea. His grace provides, in a sense, a safe passage on dry ground.

To help us remember the fullness of that blessing—to keep its memory from fading over the years—Christ gave us the sacred meal. Each time we partake of the supper, it stirs our remembrance of God's miracle, the miracle that provided a path for crossing safely into his kingdom.

MEDITATION 49

WATER FOR THE THIRSTY

Jesus answered, "Everyone who drinks this water will be thirsty again, but whoever drinks the water I give them will never thirst. Indeed, the water I give them will become in them a spring of water welling up to eternal life."

—JOHN 4:13–14

Lisa sounded bitter and forlorn as she poured out her pain. Her unhappy marriage had ended in divorce. Since then she'd had three failed live-in romances. She wondered what was wrong with her and why she couldn't sustain a lasting relationship.

Jesus came face-to-face with a woman like Lisa. He met her at a well in Samaria, and the fourth chapter of John's gospel describes their encounter.

Tired and thirsty from his journey, Jesus asked her for a drink. Her eyes widened in shocked disbelief. She was a woman, and Jews didn't speak in public to women. She also was a Samaritan, whom the Jews despised as half-breed defilers of God's law. Jews believed even using a drinking vessel handled by a Samaritan would make them unclean. Stunned, therefore, she wondered, "How can you ask me for a drink?"

Jesus said if she only knew who he was, she would ask him for a drink, and he would give her not just a cupful, but a fountain of water. He was speaking of the Holy Spirit, who would supply rivers of refreshing water bubbling up within her.

Jesus knew that to reach this woman's heart he must help her face the arid landscape of her life, so he said, "Go, call your husband, and come back."

Perhaps hoping her answer would stop his scrutiny, she replied, "I have no husband."

Jesus continued to probe her wounds and old scars. He said, "You are right when you say you have no husband. The fact is, you have had five husbands, and the man you now have is not your husband."

Ah! It's all out in the open now—the whole ugly mess of her life. She has gone through husbands like a drunkard goes through liquor bottles. And she has nothing to show for it but pain.

Jesus knew her life was empty and her spiritual well was dry. And she did too. She said, "I know that

FOOD for the JOURNEY

Messiah is coming. When he comes, he will explain everything to us." And in her mind, she must have been asking, "It couldn't be you, could it?"

But it was.

Perhaps some of this Samaritan woman lives in Lisa and in us all. But no matter how broken we are, no matter how beat-up by life we might be, no matter how parched our lives, there is still hope. The woman at the well experienced it. And after working through several issues in her life, so has Lisa.

Jesus offers us living water. And each time I take the Lord's Supper, I drink in a little more of him. Like an artesian well, the refreshing water of Christ helps quench my desperate thirst. When I come to the Lord's Table, I come with adoration for the Savior who doesn't bypass parched people like the Samaritan woman. People like Lisa. People like me. People like you.

MEDITATION 50

SEEING JESUS MORE CLEARLY

When [Jesus] was at the table with them, he took bread, gave thanks, broke it and began to give it to them. Then their eyes were opened and they recognized him, and he disappeared from their sight. They asked each other, "Were not our hearts burning within us while he talked with us on the road and opened the Scriptures to us?"
—Luke 24:30–32

Disappointment and discouragement marked the two believers who trudged the seven miles from Jerusalem to Emmaus. They had hoped Jesus would bring deliverance to Israel, but Jewish leaders sent him instead to a horrible death. So their hopes and dreams had come to a premature and bloody end.

Even the women's discovery of an empty tomb didn't lift their spirits. It only raised more questions and increased their confusion.

As the despondent disciples, Cleopas and likely his wife, Mary, tramped the dusty road to their small village, Jesus joined them, yet somehow they didn't recognize him. He asked, "What are you discussing as you walk?"

Cleopas asked, "Are you the only one visiting Jerusalem who doesn't know what has happened there in the last few days?"

"What things?"

"About Jesus of Nazareth," they replied. And they poured out their pain and bitter disappointment, adding, "We had hoped that he would be the one who would set Israel free."

Yes, they had hoped but no longer. They had stood at the bedside of hope for three days, but in the end, hope died. There had been no funeral, nothing but a sense of confusion and loss.

Have you ever experienced the death of hope? When all the doors seemed shut and barred? If so, you can understand the disillusionment and defeat that broke the spirits of these two disciples.

Jesus understood their disappointment, and so, beginning with Moses and the prophets, he explained to them what the Scriptures said about the Messiah.

With each explanation the despondency and discouragement that had weighed on them lifted like the spring winds lift the clouds. They could sense their hearts coming alive again, the fire of hope burning once more deep within.

Still not knowing who the stranger was, they urged him to stay the night, for the sun was about to set. An unexpected turn occurred when they served the evening meal. No longer the guest, Jesus assumed the role of host. He "took bread, gave thanks, broke it and began to give it to them," just as he had at the Last Supper.

Suddenly "their eyes were opened and they recognized him." Perhaps we, too, can see Jesus more clearly when we meet him at the Table.

We are all wayfarers on a pilgrimage to know Jesus more deeply. And the beauty is that he enters our story as he did for those followers on the Emmaus road. He does it when we take part in the Lord's Supper. And each time we meet him there, we catch another glimpse of who he is. At each encounter we may discern a different facet, gaining a new insight that makes our hearts sing within us.

As insightful as was the experience on the Emmaus road and as satisfying as it is when we meet Jesus in the Lord's Supper, it is only a foretaste of what we will experience when we see him face-to-face.

MEDITATION 51

Reservation Guaranteed

By his great mercy we have been born anew to a living hope through the resurrection of Jesus Christ from the dead, and to an inheritance which is imperishable, undefiled, and unfading, kept in heaven for you, who by God's power are guarded through faith for a salvation ready to be revealed in the last time.
—1 Peter 1:3–5, RSV

I recall driving south on the Alaska-Canadian highway with my family and planning to select a hotel after I got to our destination. To my dismay when we arrived all the hotels were booked solid. And towns along that highway were scarce.

From then on I have made sure to confirm all our reservations before starting a trip. It comforted my wife to know our family of five wouldn't have to sleep in the car again.

I'm grateful God has guaranteed our reservations for the inheritance he provides. I often ponder this gift during the Lord's Supper because it's the resurrection of Jesus that makes this blessing possible.

This inheritance is so spectacular that Peter can only describe it by telling us what it is not. He says our inheritance is *imperishable* because nothing can destroy it. Moths cannot eat it. Rust cannot reduce it. Thieves cannot steal it.

Our inheritance is also *undefiled*, meaning it is unstained, unspoiled, and uncontaminated.

Peter says our inheritance is *unfading*. He uses a word from which we get our word *marathon*. Our inheritance, like a marathon runner, has a lasting quality. It never loses its vitality. After we've basked in our inheritance for ten thousand years, it will still be fresh and wondrous.

This inheritance is *kept* or *reserved* in heaven for us. The Greek word is a military term meaning well guarded. God's angel army is defending our inheritance, keeping it safe, reserving it for all those who follow Christ.

Our reservations are guaranteed by God, sealed with the blood of Christ, and they have your name and mine stamped all over them.

How awesome is that?

But Peter has more to say. He states that just as God guards our inheritance, his power also guards us. Satan does his best to keep us from gaining our legacy, but he is no match for heaven's military force that is escorting us to our inheritance.

Guaranteed reservations for heaven banish our anxieties and ignite our hope. And this is not a weak "We wish" hope but a confident "We know!" hope. We *know* the Father gives us this inheritance. We are certain it is guarded by angel battalions and confident the death and resurrection of Christ guarantee our access to it.

How can we even begin to express our gratitude for these assurances?

A good starting point is for us to offer our sincere worship to the Father in the sacred moments of Communion. Our praises will warm his heart, and our gratitude will gladden his spirit.

MEDITATION 52

IT IS FINISHED!

A jar of wine vinegar was there, so they soaked a sponge in it, put the sponge on a stalk of the hyssop plant, and lifted it to Jesus's lips. When he had received the drink, Jesus said, "It is finished." With that, he bowed his head and gave up his spirit.
—JOHN 19:29–30

The apostles stood bewildered and forlorn, watching from afar as Jesus was crucified. Their Messiah was dying, and so were their hopes. All their expectations were crashing down like the walls of Jericho.

From their safe vantage point, they saw Jesus turn to one of the other victims and say something to him, but they couldn't make out his words.

Perhaps it's that way with you sometimes, as it is with me. When standing at a distance from Jesus, it's difficult to hear what he is saying.

But then Jesus shouted with a loud voice, "It is finished!" That the apostles could hear—one word in Greek, three words in English: It-is-finished.

> Concise.
> > Crisp.
> > > Neat.

But what did the Savior mean? *What* was finished?

Jesus was declaring that the work God had assigned him was now complete. God's plan for our redemption was finally realized. The strategy he formulated before the foundation of the world was at last culminated. The grand scheme of redemption so patiently woven through the ages was now accomplished. From God's calling of Abraham to the miraculous birth of Jesus and his teachings, signs, and miracles—*all of it* had reached its zenith in the crucifixion of Christ.

That's what was finished.

His cry from the cross was not the moan of the defeated, not a whispered resignation to death, but the roar of victory—the exultant cry of the Godhead! Oswald Chambers stated, "The greatest note of triumph that ever sounded in the ears of a startled universe were the words of Christ from the Cross—'It is finished.'"

So what does this mean for us as we take part in the Lord's Supper?

It means we can celebrate that Christ was not the victim but the *Victor*. He overcame the Serpent's devious strategy in Eden and the temptations in the desert. He took everything Satan threw at him, including the farce of a trial and a criminal's death. And still he won.

It means the sacred meal is a reminder that in Christ we, too, are no longer victims. The blood of Jesus has freed us and made us victorious.

It means as we take Communion, we can be confident that God's immeasurable grace has paid our debt and erased our guilt.

It means our Father is steady, unwavering through the centuries, always dependable and persistent. What he set out to do, he completed. Nothing, not even Satan himself, could deter our Father from his plan to redeem us, a people for his own possession.

He is the Lord God Almighty and worthy of our praise, especially at the Lord's Table where we participate in this most sacred act of Christian worship. It is here that we commemorate the sacrificial death of his Son and recall the last words Jesus thundered before he bowed his head in victory:

"It is finished!"

Acknowledgments

All books are shaped by a team of dedicated people. *Food for the Journey* is no different.

I am indebted to my colleagues at the Trinity Arts Writers Workshop for providing valuable critiques as I presented each of these meditations.

My gratitude extends to the faithful beta readers who gave helpful feedback. Several of them have connections to the Hills Church in Richland Hills, Texas. These include Erich Robinson, spiritual formation minister; Chris Hatchett, lead minister of the Southlake campus; former member Doug Vaughn; and Jerry Smith, who always has a smile on his face and encouragement on his lips.

Several of the beta readers share Alaskan roots with our family. These include Dana Buss, who was born in Juneau during the time we ministered there, and Linda Judd, whose wedding to Dan I officiated. Patty Slack, an author and talented editor in her own right, was also born in Alaska during our tenure. Her parents were fellow students in our Pepperdine days. Kathie Schmitz and her husband, Fred, became Christians while we lived there and have been our dear friends ever since.

Other helpful beta readers include Justin Cherry, a

Acknowledgments

missionary serving in New Zealand, and Laura Waldron, our daughter-in-law, whose soul swims in deep waters.

Matt Waldron, our son, cheered me on and provided strategic advice, for which I am grateful.

I am thankful also for Sara-Meg Seese, who edited an early version of the manuscript.

I am especially indebted to Carol Bartley, an editor par excellence, who corrected my mistakes, taught me much about writing, and has become a dear friend. My thanks also to the good folks at IntelliSmartDigital, Elm Hill Books, and HarperCollins Christian Publishing for making the book a reality.

The talented Kristen Ingebretson designed the book's cover. It was delightful working with such a congenial professional.

I am thankful also for the missionaries and fellow Christians in countries around the world who shared the Lord's Supper with me amid the richness of their respective cultures.

Most of all I am thankful for my wife, who has been an indispensable sounding board, always encouraging but, when needed, gently guiding me in other directions. She also proofread every page—through several revisions.

I am struck profoundly by the limitations of human beings who by the utter weakness of written words attempt to describe the divine. But my prayer is that God will in some way use these pages to enrich your experience of Christ during the Lord's Supper, to speak a message of transformation into your life, and ultimately bring glory to his name.

Notes

Preface

spiritual lethargy or even spiritual death:
   1 Corinthians 11:29-30.

Meditation 1: Food for the Journey

1: *the single most important provision*: Pliny, Epist. vii. 12. The ancient Greeks had the custom of providing a meal for those beginning a journey. It later included everything needed for the journey, such as money, clothes, and supplies. In Latin that meal and those provisions were called *viaticum.* Roman Catholicism applied the term to the provision for the journey of life in general. Finally it was used as "provision for the passage out of this world into the next …. **In the course of time 'viaticum' was applied to the Eucharist generally**" (emphasis added). Augustin Joseph Schulte, "Viaticum," in *The Catholic Encyclopedia* (New York: Robert Appleton, 1912), vol. 15, accessed September 22, 2019, http://www.newadvent.org/cathen/15397c.htm.

Notes

2: *a roaring lion hungering to devour*: 1 Peter 5:8.

3: *On the strength of the angel meal, Elijah "traveled forty days and forty nights"*: 1 Kings 19:8.

Meditation 2: More Than a Museum of Memories
5: *This single remarkable event ... that caught even the angels by surprise*: 1 Peter 1:10–12.

Meditation 3: A Rose by Any Other Name
8: *Picasso's full name* is Pablo Diego José Francisco de Paula Juan Nepomuceno María de los Remedios Cipriano de la Santísima Trinidad Ruiz y Picasso.

8: *"What's in a name? That which we call a rose"*: William Shakespeare, *Romeo and Juliet*, ed. G. B. Harrison (New York: Harcourt, Brace, 1948), 2.2.43–44. References are to act, scene, and line.

9: *most churches have reached considerable consensus*: N. T. Wright, *Simply Christian: Why Christianity Makes Sense* (New York: Harper One, 2006), 153.

Meditation 4: The Lord's Supper As Sacrament
10: *Perhaps in your church the word* sacrament *is rarely used*: Some today prefer "ordinance" rather than "sacrament" because of the earlier misuse of the word. But "sacrament," as I am using it, is a mystery pointing to the work of God in Christ

that is marked by three characteristics: first, it is a command of Christ; second, it celebrates his death, burial, and resurrection; and third, it requires our participation.

11: *It was required of each soldier upon his enlistment in the military*: William Barclay, *The Lord's Supper* (Louisville, KY: Westminster John Knox, 200:1), 1–2.

11: *the same was true of Christ's disciples through their regular observance of the Lord's Supper*: Tertullian, *Ad Martyres*, c. iii.

11: *We are buried with Christ in baptism, and rise...to walk in newness of life*: Romans 6:3–4, NRSV.

Meditation 5: The New Passover Lamb

14: *"from the firstborn son of Pharaoh"*: Exodus 11:5.

14: *"the Lamb of God, who takes away the sin of the world"*: John 1:29.

15: *"the blood will be a sign for you"*: Exodus 12:13.

Meditation 7: Just a Symbol?

20: *"Whenever the rainbow appears in the clouds"*: Genesis 9:16, emphasis added.

21: *"swept away your offenses like a cloud"*: Isaiah 44:22.

Notes

Meditation 9: All Loves Excelling

26: *So he prayed they would ... understand the breadth, length*: Ephesians 3:17–18.

26: *"And such were some of you"*: 1 Corinthians 6:11, RSV.

27: *Charles Wesley's hymn "Love Divine, All Loves Excelling"*: 1747.

Meditation 10: The Meal of Self-Evaluation

30: *"No one is worthy"*: Jillian Kittrell, "The Church Hasn't Changed a Bit," *The Christian Chronicle*, March 2017.

Meditation 11: His Alone

31: *God left their bleached bones scattered:* 1 Corinthians 10:3–6.

32: *"behind the nothingness of the idols"*: Allan J. McNicol, "Lord's Supper as Hermeneutical Clue: A Proposal on Theological Method," *Christian Studies,* 46 (Fall 1990), 41–54.

33: *The hymn "Pierce My Ear"*: Steve Croft, 1980. Lyrics available at hymnlyrics.org/ newlyrics_p/pierce_my_ear.php.

Meditation 12: The Table of Mercy

35: *"we have accepted an invitation engraved with the blood of God's Son"*: Allan J. McNicol, *Preparing for the Lord's Supper: Nourishing*

NOTES

Spiritual Life Through the Lord's Meal (Austin: Christian Studies Press, 200:7), 49.

Meditation 13: The Meal for Honored Guests

38: *"there were* many *who followed him"*: Mark 2:15, emphasis added.

38: *Consider his meal with Levi*: Luke 5:27–31.

38: *a parable about a wealthy man*: Luke 14:15–21.

Meditation 14: The New Moses

40: *"This cup is the new covenant"*: Luke 22:20.

40: *"This is the blood of the covenant"*: Exodus 24:8.

41: *Moses lifted the bronze snake*: Numbers 21:6–9; John 3:14–15.

41: *"baptized into Moses in the cloud and in the sea"*: 1 Corinthians 10:2.

41: *Believers today are "baptized into Christ"*: Galatians 3:27.

41: *"For I have not spoken on my own authority"*: John 12:49, RSV.

Meditation 15: Bride Prices and Ransoms

44: *"If you like, give me my wages"*: Zechariah 11:12–13, NLT.

Notes

Meditation 17: When Wild Winds Blow

50: *That's when the Holy Spirit intercedes ... "with groanings too deep for words"*: Romans 8:26, NASB.

51: *when the battles rage and wild winds blow*: Adapted from Annie Johnson Flint's poem "Better Than My Best," "Poetry by Annie Johnson Flint," Precept Austin, updated August 1, 2016, https://www.preceptaustin.org/annies_poems/.

51: *"Never will I leave you; never will I forsake you"*: Hebrews 13:5.

Meditation 18: The Covenant Meal

52: *He declares, "I will not violate my covenant"*: Psalm 89:34.

53: *The people responded, "Everything the L*ORD *has said we will do"*: Exodus 24:3.

53: *This was "the blood of the covenant"*: Exodus 24:8.

53: *they saw the God of Israel and ate and drank before him*: Exodus 24:9, 11.

53: *This ancient covenant meal*: People in Old Testament times often used covenant meals to seal a pact between two or more parties (e.g., Isaac and Abimelek, Genesis 26:28–30; Jacob and Laban, Genesis 31:44–54).

NOTES

53: *"The true talk that God said our war is over"*: Wycliffe Bible Translators, "Imbo Ungu," *In Other Words*, Spring 1999, 1.

Meditation 19: The Day of Atonement

57: *"as far as the east is from the west"*: Psalm 103:12.

Meditation 20: The Meal of Reconciliation

59: *And when both families eat this meal, forgiveness is offered*: Vincent J. Donovan, *Christianity Rediscovered*, 25th anniversary ed. (Maryknoll, NY: Orbis, 2003), 46.

Meditation 21: The High Cost of a Free Gift

62: *It's a precious gift he extends to us "freely by his grace"*: Romans 3:24.

62: *"The* free *gift of God is eternal life"*: Romans 6:23 RSV, emphasis added.

63: *They chanted, "Come down from the cross"*: Matthew 27:40.

63: *"My God, my God, why have you forsaken me"*: Matthew 27:46.

63: *"No one can redeem the life of another"*: Psalm 49:7–8

Meditation 22: The New Manna

65: *"the bread of angels"*: Psalm 78:25.

65: *"The Body of our Lord Jesus Christ"*: The Episcopal Church, *The Book of Common Prayer* (New York: Church Hymnal, 1979), 338.

Meditation 26: The Table of Tears

77: *That's when tears leak from our eyes because of our many sins*: Psalm 119:136.

77: *"Have mercy on me, O God, according to your unfailing love"*: Psalm 51:1–2.

78: *"I have heard your prayer and seen your tears; I will heal you"*: 2 Kings 20:5.

78: *"You will grieve, but your grief will turn to joy"*: John 16:20.

Meditation 27: The Meal That Nourishes

80: *"Bread of heaven, Feed me till I want no more"*: William Williams, "Guide Me, O Thou Great Jehovah," 1745.

Meditation 29: The Meal of Purity

85: *"Now the* Festival of Unleavened Bread, *called the* Passover*"*: Luke 22:1, 7, emphasis added.

86: *"For seven days no yeast is to be found"*: Exodus 12:19.

86: *"Beware of the leaven of the Pharisees and Sadducees"*: Matthew 16:6, NASB.

Notes

Meditation 30: The One-Loaf Meal

90: *"As this broken bread was scattered upon the mountains"*: *Didache*, in *The Apostolic Fathers*, trans. Kirsopp Lake, vol. 1, Loeb Classical Library (Cambridge, MA: Harvard University Press, 1975), 9:3–4.

Meditation 31: Thanksgiving and Celebration

92: *"the riches of God's grace that he lavished on us"*: Ephesians 1:7–8.

Meditation 32: The Mountains of Fear and Joy

95: *First he describes the mountain of fear*: Hebrews 12:18–21.

95: *"darkness, gloom and storm"*: Hebrews 12:18.

Meditation 33: The New Creation

98: *"Create in me a clean heart, O God"*: Psalm 51:10, NASB.

99: *That means others, including you and me, will follow*: 1 Corinthians 15:20–23.

Meditation 34: Healing the Shame

100: *Brian and his wife, Megan*: These are not their actual names.

102: *No one who believes in Christ will ever "be put to shame"*: Romans 10:11.

102: *"I broke the bars of your yoke and enabled you to walk"*: Leviticus 26:13.

NOTES

Meditation 35: Grace Reigns!

104: *Instead he pours into our lives his "abundant provision of grace"*: Romans 5:17.

104: *We are saved "by grace"*: Ephesians 2:8.

104: *"justified freely by his grace"*: Romans 3:24.

104: *"loved us and by his grace gave us eternal encouragement"*: 2 Thessalonians 2:16.

105: *"we have an advocate with the Father"*: 1 John 2:1–2.

Meditation 36: The Messianic Banquet

106: *Christians call that celebration the Messianic banquet*: "A symbolic portrayal of the blessings of the age to come in which those chosen by God share in a rich feast with the Messiah (Luke 14:15). In the NT this is often pictured as a marriage supper with Jesus Christ as the groom and the church as both bride and invited guests (Revelation 19:9). The feast, which will take place after the consummation of God's kingdom, is prefigured in the Lord's Supper (Mark 14:25; Luke 22:15–16)." Scriptures added by author. Bible Gateway, Dictionary of Bible Themes. https://www.biblegateway.com/resources/dictionary-of-bible-themes/9150-Messianic-banquet.

NOTES

106: *"I tell you, I will not drink from this fruit of the vine from now on"*: Matthew 26:29.

107: *After the Supper he added, "I confer on you a kingdom"*: Luke 22:29–30.

108: *"For seven days they celebrated with joy the Festival of Unleavened Bread"*: Ezra 6:22.

Meditation 37: The Lord's Fervent Desire

110: *"Come drink, this is my blood of the new covenant. Come eat, this is my body given for you"*: The author's paraphrase of Matthew 26:28 and Luke 22:19.

111: *"When we eat from the same plate, our love for one another is deepened"*: Victor Edwin, "A Work Desired by God," *America: The Jesuit Review*, March 21, 2005, *https://www.americamagazine.org/issue/524/article/work-desired-god*.

Meditation 38: Waiting: The Time Between

114: *The angels declared to the apostles, "This same Jesus, who has been taken from you into heaven"*: Acts 1:11.

Meditation 39: The Cosmic Battle

115: *"It's the end of the world! Go home and prepare to die"*: "Welles Scares Nation," This Day in History: October 30, 1938, History.

com, updated July 27, 2019, www.history.com/this-day-in-history/welles-scares-nation/.

Meditation 40: This Is Holy Ground

119: *"Take off your sandals, for the place where you are standing"*: Exodus 3:5; Joshua 5:15.

119: *"Surely the L*ORD* is in this place, and I was not aware of it"*: Genesis 28:16.

119: *"How awesome is this place"*: Genesis: 28:17.

Meditation 41: Betrayal at the Table

121: *"Surely you don't mean me, Rabbi"*: Matthew 26:25.

123: *"the sacrifice acceptable to God is a broken spirit"*: Psalm 51:17, RSV.

Meditation 43: For the Joy Set before Him

127: *"My soul is overwhelmed with sorrow to the point of death"*: See Matthew 26:38–42 for the events noted in this meditation.

Meditation 44: Scorning the Shame

131: *It was the shame of receiving the curse of God*: Galatians 3:13.

Meditation 45: The Kiss of Death

134: *"Why wasn't this perfume sold"*: John 12:5.

NOTES

134: *"What are you willing to give me"*: Matthew 26:15.

134: *"What you are about to do, do quickly"*: John 13:27.

135: *"Do what you came for, friend"*: Matthew 26:50.

Meditation 46: The Lord's Supper As Sacrifice

137: *Additionally, Paul charges us to present our bodies*: Romans 12:1.

138: *"as those who have been brought from death to life"*: Romans 6:13.

Meditation 47: Under His Wings

140: *"the terror of night" to "the plague that destroys at midday"*: Psalm 91:5–6.

Meditation 48: Crossing on Dry Land

143: *The ... river was at flood stage, making it a raging torrent impossible to cross*: Joshua 3:15.

Meditation 49: Water for the Thirsty

145: *Lisa sounded bitter and forlorn*: Lisa is not her actual name.

Meditation 50: Seeing Jesus More Clearly

149: *As the despondent disciples, Cleopas and likely his wife, Mary, tramped the dusty road*: N. T.

Wright, *The Meal Jesus Gave Us: Understanding Holy Communion*. Revised edition. Originally published in Great Britain (Louisville, KY: Westminster John Knox, 2014), 67.

149: *Jesus joined them, yet somehow they didn't recognize him*: Something about Jesus's resurrection body prevented people from easily recognizing him. Mary at the empty tomb did not recognize Jesus (John 20:14). Mark 16:12 says that after appearing to Mary at the tomb, "Jesus appeared *in a different form* to two of them while they were walking in the country" and they did not recognize him (emphasis added). The eleven did not realize who Jesus was when he appeared to them until they saw his wounds (Luke 24:36–41). And the seven disciples fishing on the Sea of Galilee did not at first recognize Jesus standing on the shore (John 21:1–4).

149: *Cleopas asked*: The conversation between Jesus and this couple is here paraphrased but is based on Luke 24.

Meditation 52: It Is Finished!

155: *"The greatest note of triumph that ever sounded"*: Oswald Chambers, *My Utmost for His Highest: Selections for the Year* (New York: Dodd, Meade, 1935, 1963). Selection for November 21, "It Is Finished."

Select Bibliography

Barclay, William. *The Lord's Supper.* Louisville: Westminster John Knox, 2001.

Barth, Markus. *Rediscovering the Lord's Supper: Communion with Israel, with Christ, and Among Guests.* Atlanta: John Knox, 1988.

Foley, Edward. *From Age to Age: How Christians Have Celebrated the Eucharist.* Chicago: Liturgy Training Publications, 1991.

Hicks, John Mark. *Enter the Water, Come to the Table: Baptism and the Lord's Supper in Scripture's Story of New Creation.* Abilene (TX): Abilene Christian University Press, 2014.

Hicks, John Mark. *Come to the Table: Revisioning the Lord's Supper.* Abilene, TX: Leafwood, 2002.

LaVerdiere, Eugene. *The Eucharist in the New Testament and the Early Church.* Collegeville: Minnesota: The Liturgical Press, 1996.

Lumpkin, William Latane. *Meditations for Communion Services.* Nashville: Abingdon, 1968.

Select Bibliography

McNichol, Allan J. *Preparing for the Lord's Supper: Nourishing Spiritual Life through the Lord's Meal.* Austin: Christian Studies Press, 2007.

Marshal, I. Howard. *Last Supper and Lord's Supper.* Vancouver, British Columbia: Regent College, 1980.

Moore, Russell D., I. John Hesselink, David P. Scaer and Thomas A. Baima. *Understanding Four Views on the Lord's Supper.* Church Life Counterpoints, Paul E. Engle, series editor. John H. Armstrong, general editor. Grand Rapids: Zondervan, 2007.

Murray, Andrew. [n.d., originally published 1897]. *The Lord's Table: A Help to the Right Observance of the Holy Supper.* [n.p., n.pub.].

Pitre, Brant. *Jesus and the Last Supper.* Grand Rapids: Eerdmans, 2015.

Schreiner, Thomas R. and Matthew R. Crawford. *The Lord's Supper: Remembering and proclaiming Christ until He comes.* NAC Studies in Bible and Theology. Series editor, E. Ray Clendenen, 2010.

Smith, Gordon T. *A Holy Meal: The Lord's Supper in the life of the church.* Grand Rapids: Baker Academic, 2005.

Sproul, R.C. *What Is the Lord's Supper?* Sanford, FL: Reformation Trust, 2013.

Select Bibliography

Willimon, William. *Sunday Dinner: The Lord's Supper and the Christian Life.* Nashville: The Upper Room, 1981.

Witherington, Ben III. *Making a Meal of It: Rethinking the Theology of the Lord's Supper.* Waco: Baylor University Press, 2007.

Wright, N.T. *The Meal Jesus Gave Us: Understanding Holy Communion.* Revised edition. Originally published in Great Britain. Louisville: Westminster John Knox Press, 2014.

About the Author

Born in Texas, Bob Waldron spent most of his life in Southern California, where he graduated from high school as the Outstanding Student in the Biological Sciences.

Bob attended Pepperdine University on a premed scholarship. It was there, during his freshman year, that he met Christ. And that changed his life forever. While still in school, he married Gina Piedmont, the love of his life, and began preaching for a Japanese church in Los Angeles.

He graduated with a BA in religion and later earned his masters and doctorate degrees in world missions at Abilene Christian University and Trinity Evangelical Divinity School, respectively.

At Pepperdine Bob was student body president and named Outstanding Senior in the Religion Department.

Following graduation, Bob continued ministering to the Japanese church then moved to Alaska where he preached for a church in Juneau. It was there he fell in love with rainforests, hunting, and fishing. The congregation sent him to India for three months to train village preachers. That trip reminded him of the vow he and Gina had made to serve the Lord overseas. They soon moved with their three children to Guatemala where they planted churches and trained congregational leaders.

Besides numerous journal articles, Bob coauthored *The Status of Missions*, published by Abilene Christian University Press.

Bob enjoys gardening, writing, and going on adventure trips with his son. They have canoed in the Canadian wilderness, climbed Mt. Kilimanjaro in Tanzania, and traveled 800 miles down the Amazon River on an old Brazilian stern-wheeler, with hammocks strung in the open air their only beds.

Bob and Gina now live in the Dallas/Fort Worth area and have three children, eight grandchildren, and two great-granddaughters.